Past Imperfect

Judaic Traditions in Literature, Music, and Art
Ken Frieden and Harold Bloom, *Series Editors*

Other titles in Judaic Traditions in Literature, Music, and Art

Past Imperfect

■

318 Episodes
from the Life of a Russian Artist

■

GRISHA BRUSKIN

Translated from the Russian by Alice Nakhimovsky

SYRACUSE UNIVERSITY PRESS

First Edition 2008
08 07 06 05 04 03   6 5 4 3 2 1

Previously published in Russian as volume 1 of *Proshedshee vremya nesovershennogo vida*
(Moscow: Novoe literaturnoe obozrenie, 2001).

Except where noted, all illustrations are courtesy of the author.

The paper used in this publication meets the minimum requirements of American
National Standard for Information Sciences—Permanence of Paper for Printed
Library Materials, ANSI Z39.48-1984.∞™

For a listing of books published and distributed by Syracuse University Press,
visit our Web site at SyracuseUniversityPress.syr.edu.

ISBN-13: 978-0-8156-0901-8   ISBN-10: 0-8156-0901-9

Library of Congress Cataloging-in-Publication Data
Bruskin, Grisha, 1945–
[Proshedshee vremia nesovershennogo vida. English]
Past imperfect : 318 episodes from the life of a Russian artist / Grisha Bruskin ; translated
from the Russian by Alice Nakhimovsky. — 1st ed.
p. cm. — (Judaic traditions in literature, music, and art)
"Previously published in Russian as volume 1 of Proshedshee vremya nesovershennogo vida
(Moscow: Novoe literaturnoe obozrenie, 2001)."
ISBN 978-0-8156-0901-8 (hardcover : alk. paper)   1. Bruskin, Grisha, 1945-—Anecdotes.
2. Jewish artists—Russia (Federation)—Anecdotes. I. Title.
N6999.B745A2 2008
709.2—dc22
2008008869

Manufactured in the United States of America

To my wife, Alesya,
and my friends Solomon and Marianna Volkov

GRISHA BRUSKIN was born in Moscow in 1945. His childhood unfolded in a large Jewish family and also, less benevolently, in the Stalinist and post-Stalinist Soviet state. His reputation as an important, strikingly original underground artist went international after the Sotheby's Moscow Auction of 1988, where his paintings sold for unprecedented sums. Bruskin emigrated to New York in 1988. His work has been exhibited all over the world, most recently at the Guggenheim; the Tretyakov; the Pushkin Museum of Fine Arts in Moscow; the Jewish Museum in New York; and the Reichstag in Berlin, where he has a permanent installation. He is associated with the Marlborough Gallery in New York.

■

ALICE NAKHIMOVSKY is professor of Russian and Jewish studies at Colgate University. Among her books are *Witness to History: The Photographs of Yevgeny Khaldei,* with A. D. Nakhimovsky (1997) and *Russian Jewish Literature and Identity* (1992). She is on the editorial board of the YIVO *Encyclopedia of Jews in Eastern Europe* (2008). Her most recent writing is on Russian-Jewish food and everyday life.

Contents

Grisha Bruskin's Past Imperfect
An Introduction

ALICE NAKHIMOVSKY

This book is not exactly a memoir, though it is created from memory and what it says is true. It has a number of subjects: growing up in a Jewish family in postwar Moscow, coming of age as an underground artist, emerging suddenly onto the international art scene, and traveling through the unpredictable social landscapes of Russia and the West. The memoir itself is composed of little stories, most of them less than a page, each devoted to some kind of illumination or contradiction.

The title *Past Imperfect* comes from Russian grammar. (Just after the book came out, one big Moscow book store shelved it with language textbooks.) English doesn't have an "imperfectum," but the metaphor behind both the original and the translation—an imperfect past—fits the Soviet constraints of Bruskin's childhood and his formative years as an artist. In Russian, *proshedshee vremya nesovershennogo vida* is a past that repeats without conclusion, a past you can return to and hang out in.

Because the book gives no straightforward biographical details, perhaps this is the place to do that. Grisha Bruskin was born in Moscow in 1945. He had four older sisters, making his family an unusually large one for its time and place. His father, who had just returned from the war, was a professor of engineering. His father's work and his mother's Jewish-Soviet anxieties make periodic appearances in the book, along with the preoccupations and peculiar discourse of a string of Jewish relatives on three sides of the family (his father's, his mother's, and his wife's).

The visual world in which Bruskin grew up was one of monumental Stalinist buildings and heroic statues whose message, as he would later articulate it, was: *Be like me! Be like me and you will be better!* This was the world of socialist realism, the canonic Soviet style that endeavored both to mirror reality and (without admitting the contradiction) to elevate it. Irony and ambiguity were excluded; experiment was minimal because of the requirement that art for everyone be easily understood by anyone. Bruskin's art-school education (still lifes and nudes) prepared him to create within this esthetic. But by the time he graduated, in the late 1960s, the system was starting to unravel.

At the time, of course, the unraveling was hard to see: it looked like the Soviet Union was eternal. In the art world, the official establishment maintained considerable power. The Artists Union determined who was or wasn't—in the legal sense—an artist. If you were a member, you could hope for a studio, you could take part in exhibitions, you would have access to art materials (the more seniority you had, the better). If you could afford it, you wouldn't have to hold a job. If you weren't a member and spent your days painting instead of at a job, you could be put on trial for "parasitism" and exiled somewhere remote. For these reasons artists tried to join the union, whatever their inner thoughts. Bruskin was for some years the youngest member. For him, as for many of his contemporaries, the organization was by turns absurd and threatening, though it was not a monolith and acts of kindness were possible within it.

Somewhere in the cracks of this official world was a private, unsupported, loosely connected network of nonconformist artists. Soviet nonconformist art had emerged in the years after Khruschev's secret speech of 1956, in which he denounced Stalin's crimes and set the stage for the relatively liberal period known as the Thaw. Nonconformist art suffered a setback but also got international publicity after the exhibition at the Manezh in 1962, which included a few pieces of avant-garde art. Khrushchev famously appeared at the exhibit, pronounced it "dog shit," and had, on the spot, a protracted debate with the artist Ernst Neizvestny. The next major, official exposure of Soviet nonconformist art was the Sotheby Moscow Auction of 1988. The central figure of that event—both celebrated and reviled—was Grisha Bruskin.

The underground art world before the auction developed in the atmosphere of intense social interactions characteristic of Soviet private life. Artists, poets, and their friends met in kitchens and studios, drank, and talked endlessly; they saw themselves engaged in something both forbidden and vitally important. There was heroism in resisting the system, and pathos. There were also, beginning in the late 1960s, connections with foreigners that took the place of a local art market, which, with isolated exceptions, was entirely absent. Diplomats and academics from Western countries came to studios and bought what they could take out; some became major collectors. For the Westerners, the price of a painting was cheap. A Soviet artist could live on the proceeds.

Unofficial art was eclectic. Some artists abandoned socialist realism for abstraction. Others worked within a framework of conceptualism, creating art in which the idea and its interpretation were preeminent. Among conceptualists, the flashiest, in pop-art terms, are the creators of "Sots Art," who turned the official Soviet visual language of socialist realism (*Sots-realizm*) into an object of parody. Bruskin's path was different. While he also uses a Soviet visual language (as well as other visual languages, some Jewish, some mystical, some invented), he is concerned above all with the mystery of the individual in a world of symbols. When he began, the powerful and repressive Soviet state was omnipresent, molding the individual through images and slogans. Now it is gone. Bruskin treats it as a lost civilization whose artifact-symbols, his creations, can be contemplated like the unearthed vases of Greece or Rome. Their provenance is recognizable. But they are, at the same time, personal to him: collective symbols distilled through the artist's imagination.

Exactly how innovative Bruskin was became clear in the course of the Sotheby auction. The auction was epoch-shattering not only because it represented the first large-scale, open interaction of the Western art market with Soviet official and nonofficial art, but also because of the upheaval in value systems that resulted. The Soviet official world had its artistic preferences, in which the Western world was uninterested. The unofficial world had its private hierarchies. Sotheby's, following its own counsel, put Bruskin's *Fundamental*

Lexicon on its catalogue cover. That painting, along with five other paintings by Bruskin, sold for just under a million dollars. The magnitude of the sum was a surprise all around. Soviet officials found the choice offensive (even as they took the money). The number of Bruskin's friends suddenly diminished. The artist himself found it hard to believe:

> Late at night after the auction . . . my wife and I found five rubles on the street.
>   Alesya asked me:
> "Should we pick it up or are we already rich?"
> I answered:
> "Take it just in case."

Bruskin emigrated to New York in 1988, joined the Marlborough Gallery, and has exhibited internationally—including many exhibitions in Russia—ever since. In 1999, he was one of four artists, each a representative of an Allied power, honored with a permanent installation at the reopened Reichstag in Berlin. Visitors to the Guggenheim's 2005 show "Russia! Nine Hundred Years of Masterpieces and Master Collections" may remember his large stainless-steel sculpture of a Pioneer—a Soviet boy scout—with his submissively blank face and, behind his back, a pair of anxiously clenched fists.

Art

Readers who approach Bruskin's writing without knowing his art might find it helpful to understand that art in a little more detail. Two themes stand out: a Soviet theme, which explores the individual in the repressive state, and a Jewish theme, which posits the individual in a world of symbol and text. As the titles of his works suggest (A *Fundamental Lexicon, Alphabetic Truths, Alefbet,)* he sees himself as creating dictionaries of images. The same types, human and demonic, appear as sculptures (displayed in groups, they don't quite interact but inhabit the same imaginative space) and as paintings, when the physical space behind them is as unreal as in an icon. Very often, the background is text, an allusion to the foundational texts that, in different ways, direct behavior in these mythic worlds.

The figures who inhabit the totalitarian world are representations of Soviet ideals (the military man, the girl athlete), though sometimes demons are among them. When they are very large, they embody a banality raised to monstrous proportions. They are pale but are portrayed with some kind of brightly colored "accessory" that corresponds to their official selves: a little girl in a costume with rabbit's ears holds a wand with a Soviet emblem; a boy's face is obscured by a portrait of the child Lenin. Their faces are blank, but they also seem trapped and lonely; they are not smiling, they are standing in certain ways because they have been put there. They bear a certain resemblance to figures from a series of painted porcelain plates called *Alphabetic Truths,* who often wear gas masks and resemble illustrations from civil defense manuals. These figures are doing what they have to do in a world that is clearly monstrous, although what exactly is going on is not explained: while each plate has a sentence written along its edge, the correspondence between word and picture is a mystery.

Critics have often pointed to the resemblance between the Soviet and Jewish themes in Bruskin's art. Both Communism and Judaism (or, for that matter, Christianity) are belief systems based on texts. But in Bruskin's work, the Soviet and Jewish themes are not really parallel. The Jewish figures in Bruskin's paintings are not modern. Their dress is Eastern European–medieval; their accessories are biblical or mystical. While their faces have a little of the distance of faces on icons—they are iconic, after all—they are not blanks. Some are mournful, some are perhaps a little crazed; their symbolic world has demons in it, but it also has tenderness. Once again, we are invited to interpret. Take what seems to be a representation of Abraham from the series *Alefbet 2* of 1984. We see him from behind—a modern little *kippa* on a round bald head—lifting a weighty ram with a thoughtful human-ish face. Some words are crossed out. A haunting image demands interpretation but doesn't quite permit it.

Memoirs

Given the text-centered nature of Bruskin's paintings, and the centrality of reading and interpretation in his education and the way he views the world, it is not surprising to see him step forward as a writer. What is, perhaps, surprising is how good he is.

Past Imperfect (2001) is the first volume of a trilogy. The three books of memoirs cover the same overlapping themes of Russia, art, and family. Each is composed of small related texts, but otherwise the manner and construction are quite different. *Yours Truly* (*Myslimo vami,* 2003) focuses on reassembling a civilization that is no longer present: the world of Grisha and Aleksandra Bruskin's grandparents and great-grandparents. The book is a dialogue between artifacts and interpretation. As you open each page, you see family photographs, letters, or postcards; opposite is a commentary that knows its own limitations and, in addition, can be read as blank verse.

The commentary stresses interpretation, but also the limits of interpretation. We are intrigued, for example, by a love story, but can never know what really happened. We can guess why a Soviet commissar, ready to leave Jewishness behind, named his daughter Safo instead of Shulamith, and knowing the hand that history dealt people like him, we can agree with Bruskin that he must have killed himself to shield his family from the consequences of a probable arrest. The commentary leads us to family secrets, like the background of shtetl wealth that was not only incompatible with Soviet myths of origin but was also dangerous.

The third volume is called *Details Follow* (*Podrobnosti pis'mom,* 2005). This book is not at all "linear": you can open it anywhere. It takes on a variety of genres: the dictionary-reference guide, the oral tale, and, briefly and engagingly, the Soviet-style guest book in which visitors sure of their standards have nothing to hide:

Dear friend! Thank you for describing my whole life.
V. Skoblikova, an old woman.

Primitive, a bunch of lies.
A Muscovite.

Tell the truth: how did you put this together?
Moscow Art Institute student

We, pupils of School 325, city of Bykov, Moscow Region, thank the
artist for his engaging excursion into the world of color and form.
Pupils of School 325

An important focus of the book is on misreadings of the cultural
code after social upheaval or immigration. In Moscow, pretty Russian
schoolgirls turn out to be prostitutes. In New York, two curators, a
Russian and an American, go to a French restaurant with what turns
out to be an odd clientele; the next day a newspaper headline reads
"Russians favor sado-maso place." As always in a Russian context,
ethnic issues loom:

> A friend in Moscow bought a copy of *Past Imperfect.*
> She went to see her girlfriend, the wife of an artist.
> The girlfriend read the blurb and called out to her husband, "Do
> you know the famous Russian artist Grisha Bruskin?"
> "First of all, he's not Russian," declared an annoyed voice from the
> next room.
> There was no "second of all."

Or further:

> The book was about to go to print.
> I called the publishing house from New York.
> I ask:
> "What's on the cover?"
> "A photo of an old Jew," said the editor, Evgeny Shklovsky.
> It was a picture of me in my youth.

In contrast to the art, and indeed the other two books in the
trilogy, *Past Imperfect* is not about interpretation. Its playful stories
often announce themselves with long titles—comically out of pro-
portion to the rest of the text—that provide a completely plausible

meaning, if often a wry one. Tiny stories in a comic-grotesque mode have an important literary antecedent in the absurdist prose of Daniil Kharms. Kharms's work from the late 1920s and 1930s began to circulate in typescript at about the time that Bruskin began painting. The influence, which Bruskin has talked about, is indirect. Unlike Kharms's deadpan "happenings," which mingle Soviet realia with grotesque fantasy and sometimes religious faith, Bruskin's little stories are based strictly on what he saw and did. They are rooted in the kind of personal stories that people in the waning years of the Soviet Union—people who knew things around them were strange—told each other as a way of asserting their verbal superiority over a world they could not control.

Of the many thematic chains that link the stories together, perhaps the most striking is the Soviet belief that permeates the ordinary world of this remembered childhood. When Bruskin is caught in a childish lie, his father comments that he's a "petty saboteur"; the comment may itself have been ironic, but the mingling of childish behavior with political, even sinister, language is still startling. In a similar mode is the story about how he discovered he was an artist, called "I Started Believing in Myself."

> In my childhood I thought there were two gods: Lenin and Stalin.
> Stalin was nevertheless the more important.
> Seeing a portrait of the Father of Nations in the newspaper, I carefully copied it in ordinary pencil into my album.
> My family, viewing this masterpiece, first identified my talent.
> I started believing in myself.

Here we have an unpredictable loop from believing in Stalin to turning into an artist and "believing in myself." The omnipresent Stalin appears in a child's perspective; the larger irony is of course an adult one.

The stories about the underground art world start in the Brezhnev era, when Communism seemed eternal and the art establishment, supported by the KGB, did its best to suppress a provocative coalition of artists, writers, and dissidents. The opportunity to test the rules blossomed under Gorbachev. The chain of stories beginning with "Regenerated Precepts" tells about the opening of Moscow's first independent alternative art exhibition, a provocation timed by the artists to coincide with an international peace conference organized by Gorbachev. Gorbachev could not have foreseen the clash between the values of his celebrity guests—people like Miloš Forman—and those of the ideological establishment, which tried to suppress the exhibition by invoking old tactics that were, by then, as pathetic as they were threatening. Soon after came the Sotheby's exhibition, with topsy-turvy consequences that included Bruskin's first trip to America.

Alongside the Soviet theme is the theme of growing up Jewish. Even in a Jewish household—even in a household where relatives, when they got together and were absolutely alone, would eat Jewish food and sing Yiddish songs—the fact of being Jewish was a little shameful. Children, like Bruskin in these stories, were shielded from the knowledge. When they found out they were Jewish, the label (as in the story below) was a kind of curse without historical or cultural meaning:

> Out on a walk I was paired with a nice little girl named Katya.
> She got mad at me and called me a Jew.
> Seeing my reaction, she said:
> "What are you so upset about? Jew and Stupidhead, they're the same thing."

The stories about Jewish self-discovery are well told here because, as in real life, the pivotal moment is always embedded in something else. In the story "At Recess," a girl gets hold of the teacher's roll book, which records everybody's ethnic background, and reads those charged words so everyone can hear; when the class resumes, the narrator could tell that "the girls [are] looking at me differently." Recognition isn't always bad: at summer camp, he's asked point-blank if he's a Jew; when he affirms it, terrified, he's given a piece of candy "for being honest."

Later, he pays attention to the subtle marks that define being a Jew despite the Soviet repression. Take, for example, the story below, called "You Wouldn't Understand This," which sketches out in minimalist but precise detail the relations between New Jew, Old Jew, and non-Jew in a Soviet postwar context. The narrator is traveling through Ukraine. His new interest in his Jewish background leads him on a search for Jewish books:

> A few days later I found myself back in Ovruch.
>
> I went into a rickety old shoe store. On the shelves were heaps of shiny black galoshes with red linings.
>
> Behind the counter was an old Jew in a hat and jacket, shooting the breeze with a Ukrainian peasant woman.
>
> I said hello and asked if he could sell me a Talmud.
>
> Figuring this was a provocation, the salesman stood up straight and said in a loud voice:
>
> "I fought in the war and was given the Order of the Red Star."
>
> From which I understood that, apparently, he did not have a Talmud.
>
> The uncomprehending peasant woman asked what we were talking about.
>
> "Oh! You wouldn't understand this!" exclaimed the veteran in a heavy Jewish accent.

So it is that two Jews, one scared and one seeking, understand each other.

As Bruskin grows older, childhood shame is replaced with curiosity and tenderness: he realizes that his family represents "the remnants of Jewish Pompeii" and seeks to preserve those remnants as best he can. His first way is through his art, where he imagines mystical Jews and their symbolic lives. His next way—a mimetic way, suffused with tenderness as well as irony—is this volume.

· · ·

Some of the stories that appeared in the Russian edition have been omitted from this English edition. Some of the wordplay just does not lend itself to translation.

Past Imperfect

A Wellspring

In my youth, reading my favorite books, I'd often think:

"What incredibly vivid and eventful childhoods these lucky authors had. A wellspring for literary creation."

I considered:

"If suddenly I decide to write a book, what can I take from my commonplace, standard-issue early life?"

Nyurka

We had a young housemaid named Nyurka.

Every morning Nyurka would wash and dress me.

One day, seeing that my sheet was wet, she threatened to reveal everything to a little girl named Dida, who had been invited that evening to my birthday party. I screamed and pulled her hair.

After that we fought each other every morning.

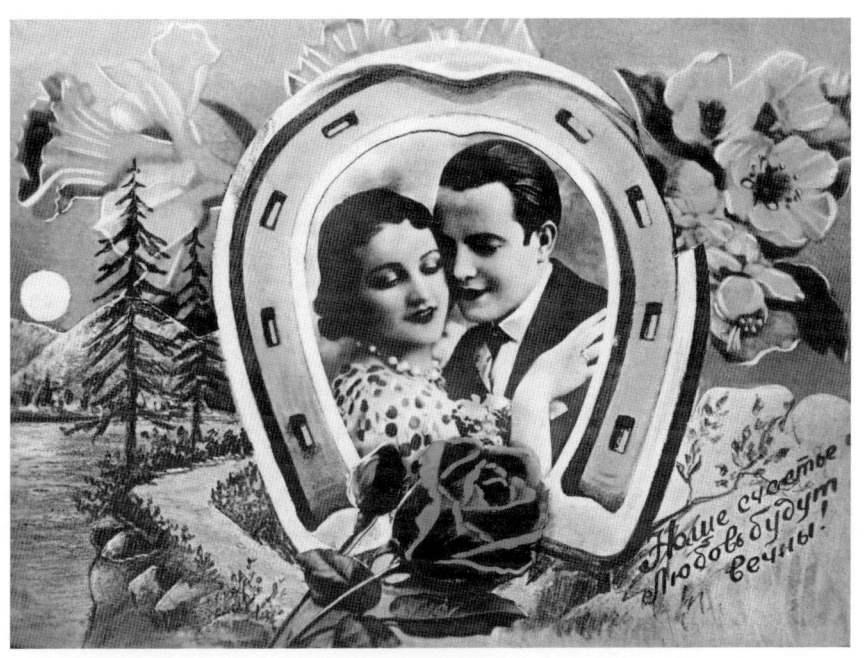

Nyurka's postcard.

Through the Iron Grille

Professor Karl Krug died. He lived one floor below us.

Nyurka decided that it was important for a child to see a dead man.

From above, through the staircase's iron grille, I saw them carry out the coffin.

In the coffin, immobile, lay a man with a white face, surrounded by flowers. Around him huddled weeping relatives.

Back in the apartment, I started pestering my family with endless questions.

To my amazement, the grown-ups couldn't answer all of them.

A Postcard for Remembrance

One day Nyurka went on a tryst with a soldier, leaving me alone in the sandbox.

An enormous German shepherd with an iron muzzle—its name was Douglas—jumped over me.

I thought it was a wolf and lost my power of speech.

For two years after that I went to a special school to get my speech back.

When my parents discovered that I was mute, they fired Nyurka.

Saying good-bye, we hugged each other and cried. Nyurka gave me a postcard, painted in bright aniline paints, to remember her by.

I still have it.

I Wanted to Be Like Everybody Else

Until I was five I didn't know I was a Jew. Then the little boys in the courtyard started teasing me.

Complaining to Mama, I learned to my sorrow that I really was a Jew, and that so were Mama and Papa, and even Grandma and my four sisters.

I wanted to be like everybody else.

But everybody else was unwilling to accept me as one of them.

A Petty Saboteur

One morning I put on a clean pair of dark brown ribbed leggings.

Deftly I fastened the elastics to the garters. Then I took a pair of scissors and cut out neat holes of varying dimensions.

"You made holes in your new leggings again!" fumed Mama.

"Mama, honestly, they tore that way," I lied shamelessly.

Mama didn't believe me.

"A petty saboteur," remarked Father in the spirit of the time.

Betrayal

In nursery school I fell in love with a girl with ash-blond hair. Her name was Natasha.

Unable to think up anything better, I proposed that we take down our pants together and compare notes.

We were discovered and severely punished. Instead of playing and enjoying ourselves, we had to spend the whole day in the nursery bedroom, on our separate cots.

Natasha snitched to the teacher that I started it and stopped talking to me.

That was the first betrayal of my life.

I suffered greatly.

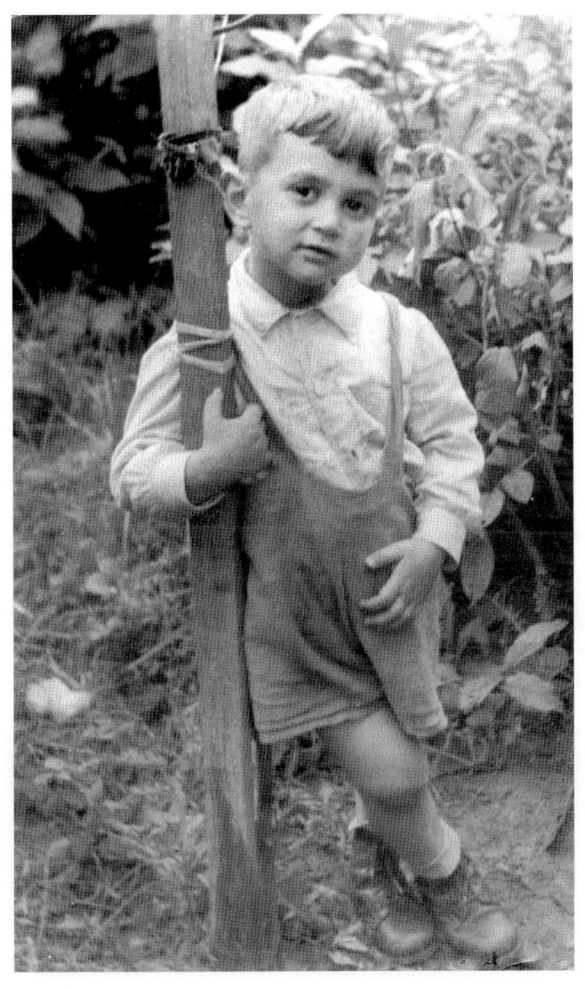

Age four, Moscow, 1949.

Out on a Walk

Out on a walk I was paired with a nice little girl named Katya.

She got mad at me and called me a Jew.

Seeing my reaction, she said:

"What are you so upset about? Jew and Stupidhead, they're the same thing."

Rags to Go!

"Rags to go!" yelled the voice from the street.

The grown-ups threw the man with the sack all sorts of rubbish. The children carried out to the courtyard anything they could.

The ragman gave the girls little copper rings.

I imagined how late at night the old man would take off his tattered clothes. He'd turn on the light. And remove his rag-tag acquisitions from the sack.

Gold coins shine in the junk pile.

Precious stones sparkle.

Reading Pinocchio

Reading *Pinocchio*, I discovered the "Land of Fools" and in that instant encountered America.

Who would have thought that someday I would settle there?

My Heart Stopped

I had been playing. Screaming, I ran into Father's study, clearly bothering him at work.

Papa put down his manuscript, took out a pistol, aimed it at me, and said:

"If you don't get out of here, I'll shoot."

I felt my heart stop from fear.

Did this really happen?

Aladdin's Cave

When I was five Father took me to Leningrad.

We went to the Hermitage.

I was ecstatic, feeling myself in Aladdin's magic cave.

Soon I needed to go to the bathroom. We ran for the exit. Past us flew treasures, armor, paintings.

"Papa, will we come back?" I asked, running.

We didn't come back. The film broke off.

I was fascinated.

So began my interest in art.

I Started Believing in Myself

In my childhood I thought there were two gods: Lenin and Stalin.

Stalin was nevertheless the more important.

Seeing a portrait of the Father of Nations in the newspaper, I carefully copied it in ordinary pencil into my album.

My family, viewing this masterpiece, first identified my talent.

I started believing in myself.

Holy Spirit

One day my father said he would show me Stalin.

He lifted me onto his shoulders and off we went to the May Day Parade.

In Red Square I felt that the Leader had looked at me.

My wife had worse luck. Her Papa, Yury Georgievich, had also decided to merge his children with the people by showing them the military parade.

The Holy Spirit did not permit this to transpire: no sooner did they leave the house than a pigeon dirtied Papa's hat.

Unity with the masses was not achieved.

They returned home.

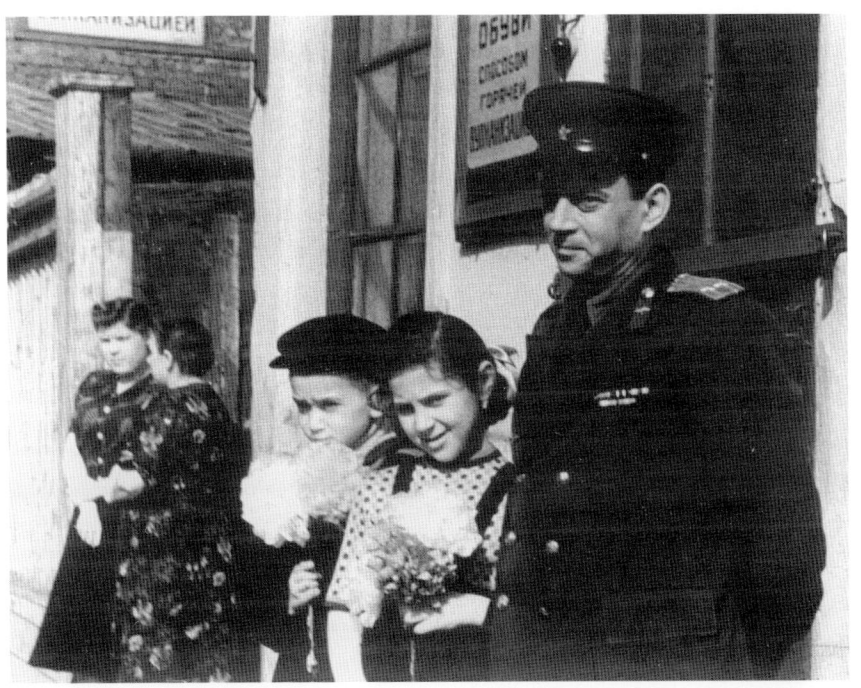

With my sister Lera and my father, Moscow, 1952.

Puppet Sunday

The most magical game of my childhood was a puppet theater.

Chasing me out of the room, my sisters would put up curtains. When all was ready, I—the sole member of the audience—was allowed in and perched on a chair.

Entry backstage was strictly forbidden.

The performance would begin.

Familiar toys, including a seriously tattered doll my father had brought from Germany, would come to life.

On the one hand, I understood that what was happening behind the scenes was a deception arranged by my sisters.

On the other hand, before me was a wonderful puppet Sunday.

I fell into confusion.

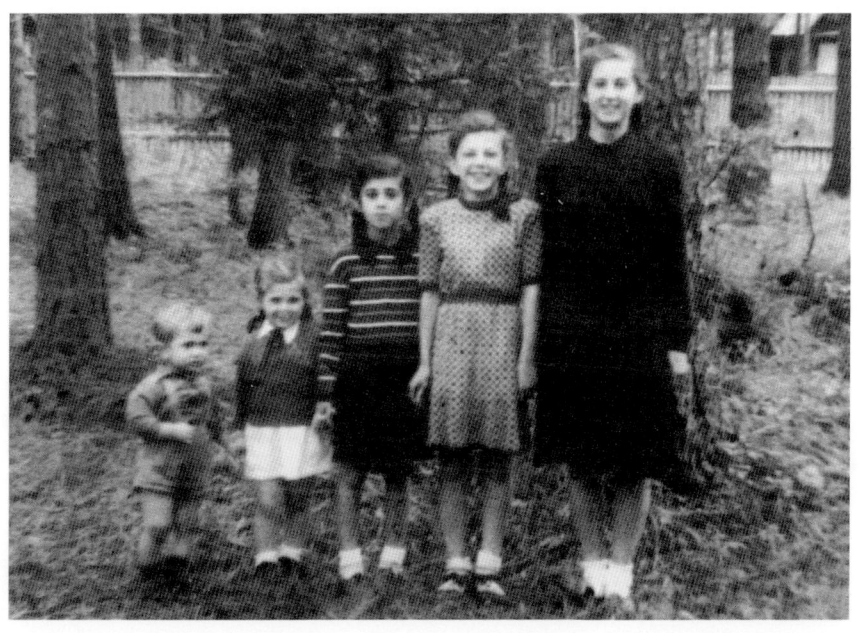

With my sisters, October 26, 1947.

A Ribbon on the Head

When they got bored with dolls, my sisters turned to me.

Outfitting me in one of their finest dresses, they tied a pretty ribbon on my head.

Later, when I read Freud, I understood that I was at risk of becoming homosexual.

My Ideal

My parents enrolled me in school.

In the schoolyard we were greeted by a woman with a noble-looking gray bun and a knitted shawl thrown over her shoulders.

My teacher's name was Marya Ivanova (to us, Marivanna).

I loved her passionately. Marivanna was my ideal. Nobody on earth was wiser, kinder, or more beautiful.

In second grade, Marivanna dyed her hair an unsuccessful brown.

My ideal dimmed, transformed instantaneously into a stupid, mean, semiliterate auntie with tiny needlelike eyes and a sharp protruding nose.

One Day

One day early in the morning our neighbor Lyalya came running over.

All in tears, she sobbed that Stalin was dead and that tomorrow there would be a war. The enemy, knowing that nobody could protect us now, would immediately seize the opportunity.

School was canceled.

At Recess

In second grade, girls and boys were put together.

Right away I fell in love.

At recess, the little girls, including the object of my secret long-ings, crowded around the class register that Marivanna had forgotten on her desk.

Looking at the very end, which held the biographical records of each pupil, they called out:

"Barinov, Russian!"

"Yashin, Russian!"

"Nazarov, Tatar!"

"Seyfulin, Tatar!"

Holding my breath, I stood at the door and watched.

"Bruskin, Jew!"

The bell rang. I walked into the classroom, and it seemed to me that the little girls were looking at me differently.

The Poet

In fourth grade it occurred to me:

"A person in love has to write poems."

I got myself a thick notebook and churned out two dozen, briskly rhyming words like "love" and "dove."

Reading the collection over, I added for depth a poem about Leningrad, which I had visited as a five-year-old.

It was not bad.

In ninth grade I came across the treasured notebook.

Full of shame, I destroyed it.

And This Is a Raphael

The men of my childhood were mostly officers in the army.

It was extraordinarily difficult to demobilize.

The artist Mitya Lion used to say that it took him half a lifetime to get out of his epaulets.

My father also wore a uniform. When he came back from Berlin after the war, he brought a car with him, a cherry-colored Opel Kapitan.

Once he took me with him on some business with his boss, the academician Colonel-General Kulebyakin. The general's house was full of paintings, drawings, and sculptures.

"Here is a Leonardo da Vinci," explained the general.

"And this is a Raphael."

My Life's Wish

At the tender age of six, I was dispatched to Pioneer Camp.

To comfort me, my father gave me my life's wish: a military canteen.

The day after I got there I took out the canteen and decided to have a drink.

Screwing off the top of the priceless gift, I reeled backwards: somebody evil had filled it to the very top with urine.

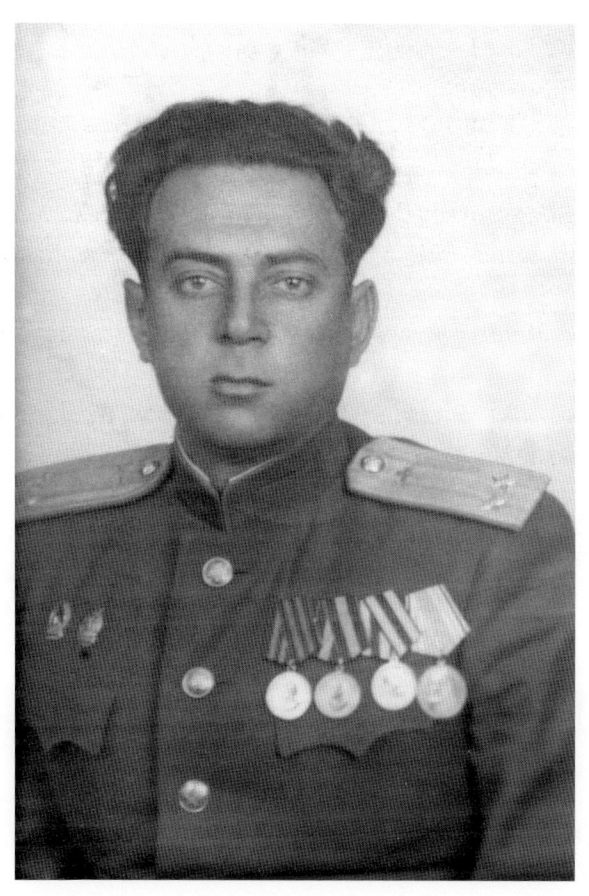

My father, 1953.

He Didn't Believe It Either

After lights out, the boys would eagerly explain to each other how children are made.

Following Mama's advice for behavior in such situations, I chose a boy who looked like he was from a good family and said to him:

"I don't believe that story. Do you?"

He didn't believe it either.

We started hanging out together.

For Being Honest

In camp I made friends with a boy my age, my distant cousin Lyonka.

One day Lyonka and I were having fun on the merry-go-round. Suddenly we were surrounded by "tough guys" from the older group.

The leader, who had a tattoo, an ex-con, in our opinion, marched up to us and, in a voice boding no good, inquired:

"Jews?"

I understood that if we said "yes," we'd be killed on the spot.

If we said "no," we would be shamed for the rest of our lives.

Preparing myself for death, cold with horror, I opened my mouth.

"Yes."

The ex-con reached into his pocket and gave me a candy.

"This is for being honest."

Torture

My father taught at the Moscow Energy Institute.

Once, when there was nobody to look after me, he took me with him to work.

We entered a hideous building: along the walls were display cases with innumerable unpleasant instruments and dials. The air had a disgusting metallic smell.

In the center of the hall was the huge cabin of a bomber. Lifting me into the pilot's seat, Papa said:

"If you press this red button, everything will blow up." Then he left to give his lecture.

Rooted to the spot, I sat there for the entire hour, staring at the dreadful button, overcoming the desire to push it.

I barely managed.

Curly-Haired, Chocolate-Colored

I very much wanted to see a real-life, curly-haired, chocolate-colored black man.

My dream came true.

Wearing a suit and hat, the overseas "comrade" floated past me, an inch away, on our ordinary Kazakov Street. Delirious with joy, I ran home.

The grown-ups for some reason were unmoved by this marvel.

Green

Many years later, a black man came to our house.

Our son took a liking to this nice guest, and they played games together for a few hours.

Eventually Tyoma got tired, looked the black man in the eye, and asked:

"And now turn green."

A Terrible Disease

At a certain age, to my surprise, I began to feel an unusual animation and discomfort in my shorts.

I decided that I had come down with a terrible disease and was about to die.

I didn't have the courage to talk to my father.

About Birds and Bees

Searching through the library, I found a book by the educator Makarenko.

Makarenko recommended to every father that he discuss delicate topics with his son when the latter reached sixteen.

I thought:

"This will be funny! Papa will tell me about birds and bees. And I've known everything for a long time."

No doubt sensing how well-informed I was, Father never in his lifetime initiated such a conversation.

Traces of War

The war inflamed the imagination of the children of my generation.

Its traces were everywhere.

In the children's camp near Moscow where I spent summers, sappers would come with minesweepers and ferret out the unexploded German mines. In the woods you could find dugouts, pillboxes, military helmets.

Most children's books and movies were about the war and featured German spies.

"German" and "Nazi" were synonyms.

I was genuinely sorry that the war was over, and I couldn't show what a brave and fearless hero I was.

The Dream

My head full of stories, I often dreamed of a field full of dead Russian soldiers.

I alone remain alive but I pretend to be dead, hoping that when darkness falls I can crawl into the forest. Germans rustle through the field, among the corpses, searching for gold teeth. I am only a boy, with all my own teeth, but by the rules of my dream to open my mouth means treason. I hope no one will notice. Suddenly through closed eyes I see the tops of high boots.

I wake up in a cold sweat.

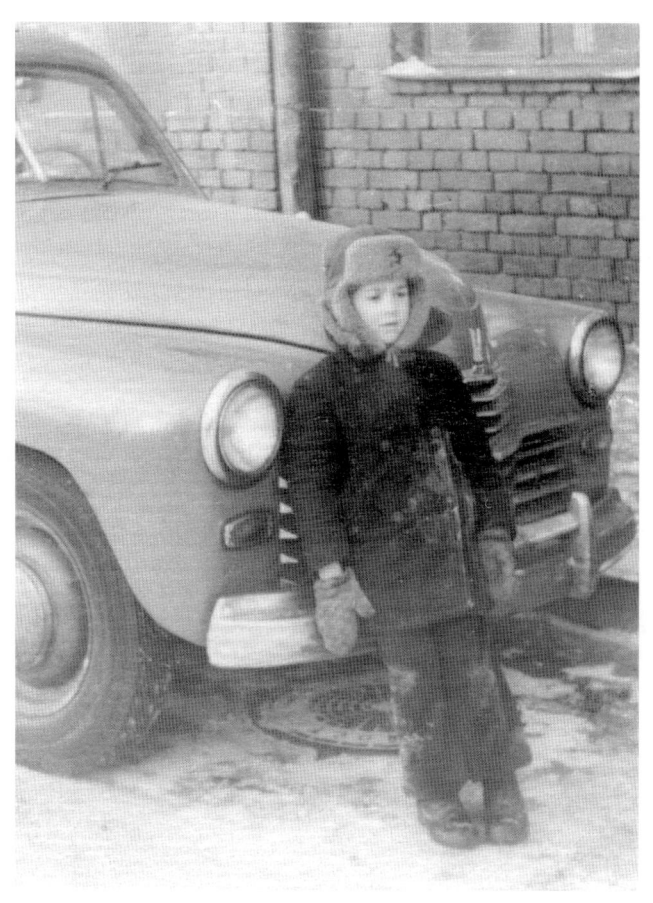

Moscow, 1953.

The Team's Commander-in-Chief

In the park opposite the house where I was born was the Stalin Sports Institute.

In the middle of a bed of pansies towered the steel figure of the Leader.

Encircling the "Sportsman's Best Friend" and everywhere in the park were dozens of sculptures depicting Soviet athletes.

In my childhood I imagined Stalin as the team's commander-in-chief.

They Still Looked Like Germans

The sculptures had been made by German prisoners of war.

Nazi and Soviet sculpture were very similar. With no need to retrain, the artists easily coped with their assignment.

But the athletes still looked like Germans.

The Language of the Enemy

At school they taught German and English.

As a postwar child, I was ready to study absolutely anything except the language of the enemy.

The "German lady" was a beautiful, stylishly dressed woman, Natalya Konstantinovna Heifetz, a family friend. Her husband had been killed at the front. She won my mother's highest regard for not remarrying and for keeping her Jewish husband's last name, even though she herself was Russian.

My father found it awkward to hand me over to the unknown "English lady."

That's how I started studying German.

Get Your Hand Out of Your Pocket!

In fifth grade we got a new homeroom teacher, the mathematician Pyotr Petrovich.

He wore a military-style jacket and nagged us indefatigably:

"Barinov, get your hand out of your pocket!"

"Seyfulin, if I see your hand in your pocket one more time, you're going into the corner."

"Bruskin, keeping your hand in your pocket is bad for you."

I couldn't figure out what the teacher had in mind.

A New Curse

At the beginning of winter the stadium of the Sports Institute became a magnificent skating rink.

Fastening blades on my felt boots, I'd grab the cigarettes I'd stolen from my father and go for a skate.

Inhaling in the frosty air would make my head spin.

It was 1956. There was a war in the Middle East.

From a kid named Izmail I heard a new curse directed at my own person: "Israel."

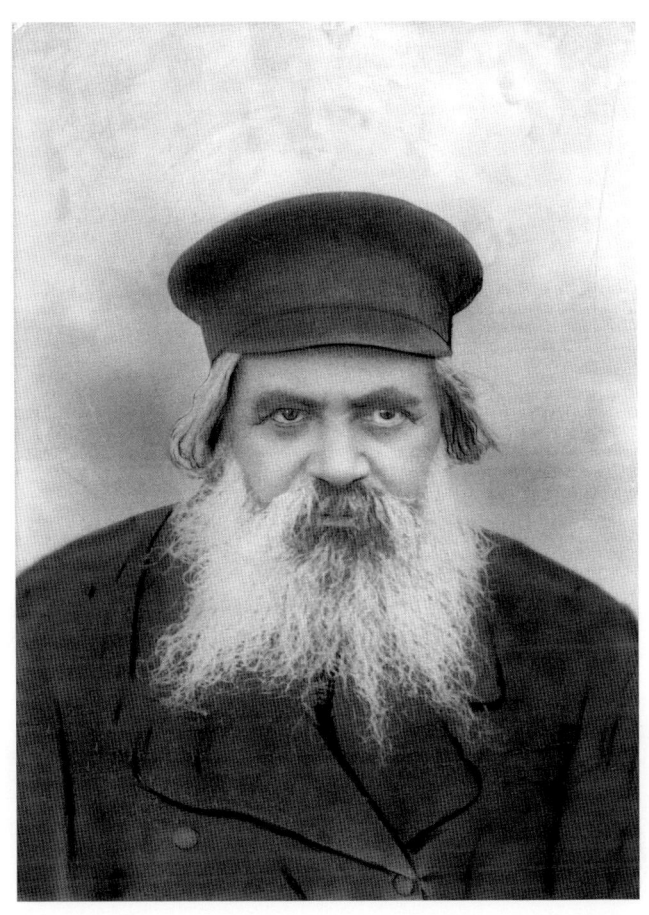

My great-grandfather.

Grandma, Do You Believe in God?

In my childhood we lived together with Grandma.

Religious traditions were not observed.

All the same, Grandma always hid away some matzo, baked under the supervision of Moscow rabbi Fishman; this was given out to the grandchildren as a treat.

There were five of us. On Friday evenings we'd start badgering her.

"Grandma, turn on the light. It's kind of dark in here."

"Let's go out and buy some ice cream."

"You know, Aunt Rosa called. She asked you to call back. Here's the telephone."

"Grandma, do you believe in God?"

Grandma smiled, remained motionless.

And didn't answer.

The Gold Ring

When she was five, Mama lived through a Jewish pogrom in Yelets.

From the window of her hiding place, she saw a Cossack demand a gold ring from her aunt's hand.

The ring fit snugly.

Too impatient to wait, the Cossack flashed his sword and cut off the finger.

Remembering this, Mama would get distraught and cry.

Grisha, Are You Still Drawing?

On holidays and birthdays, Papa the patriarch would assemble the relatives.

The next day, Mama would tell somebody on the phone:

"It was just family. Around forty people."

My grandmas and my aunts would appear in silk dresses, wearing lipstick and brooches.

Aunt Musya would come from Malakhovka, and, full of tenderness, aim to pinch my cheek, painfully, in the Jewish fashion. I hid from her in the far reaches of the apartment.

Throughout my childhood, and even when I was well past thirty, Musya never failed to inquire:

"Grisha, are you still drawing?"

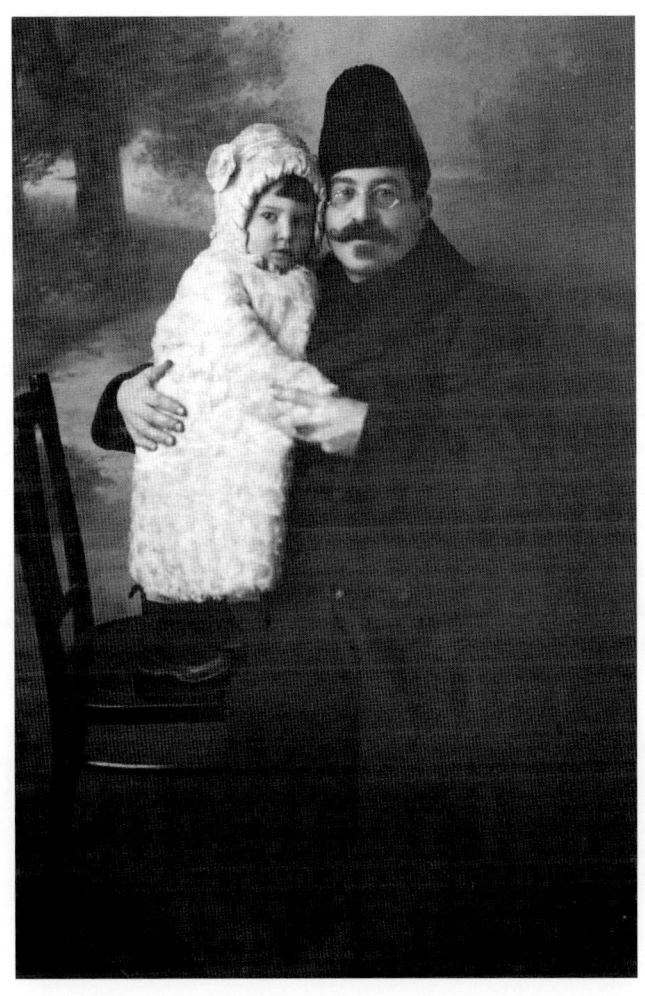

My mother with her father, Elets, 1912.

The Unearthly Beauty of Aunt Sarah

Also present were: crazy Aunt Bella with the face of King Lear and a gray "crow's nest" on her head; Uncle David the stamp collector; Uncle Yoska the loser lawyer; and Uncle Borya the honest naval officer, who liked a serious conversation about art.

From inside the door you could hear the little rustling steps of tiny Aunt Rosa, arriving on her ailing legs: this was Grandma's youngest sister.

From Leningrad came my beloved Aunt Hannah, and so on ad infinitum.

Grandpa Iosif would read a poem specially composed for the occasion.

Father, like a master of ceremonies, presided at the head of the table. And everyone would remember the unearthly beauty of Aunt Sarah, whom, by general consensus, "all Israel would have paid to see."

Sometimes, to my horror, the relatives would launch into a Yiddish song.

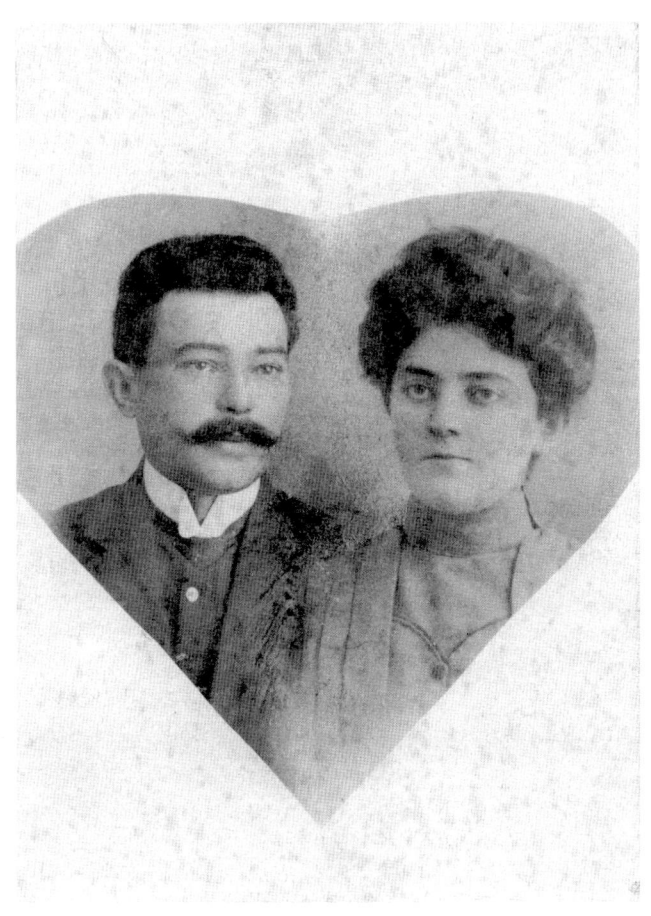

My paternal grandparents.

The Remnants of the Jewish Pompeii

When I was young I didn't like those evenings.

Embarrassed by the shtetl demeanor of the guests, I felt that I had nothing in common with them and tried to get out of the house.

Later I took pleasure in these gatherings of the remnants of the Jewish Pompeii.

I never did find anything we had in common. But I grew up, and "Pompeii" began to interest me for its own sake. I took on the role of ethnographer.

When my wife made her first appearance at one of these family saturnalias, Aunt Dora, learning how old she was, exclaimed:

"So where were you keeping yourself all this time, in a refrigerator?"

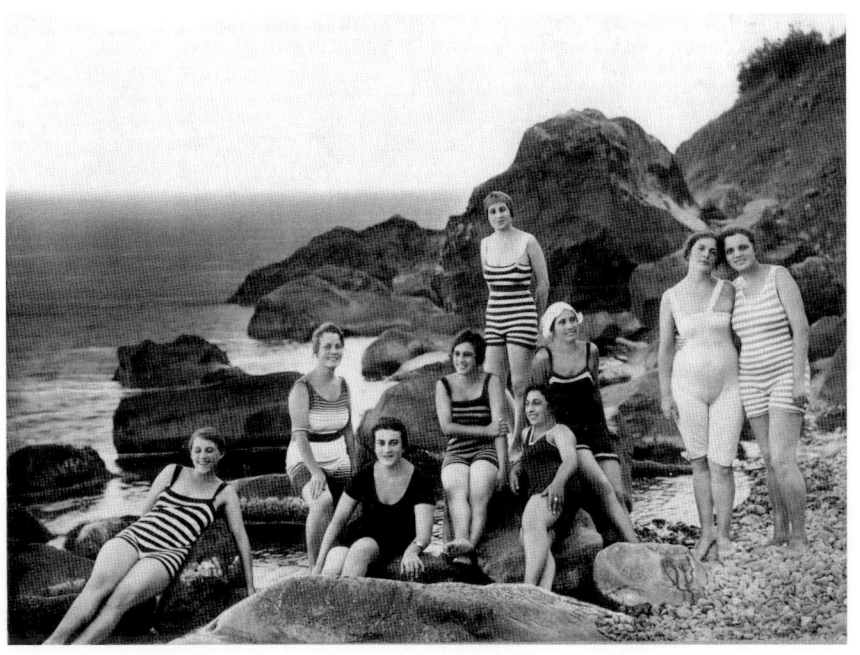

Grandma Rebecca is the second from the right, 1923.

I'd Be So Dumb

When I asked Aunt Rosa if I could paint her portrait, she said:
"You can't believe I'd be so dumb as to agree to this."

Jews and Kikes

One summer we rented a dacha in Kratovo.

In the same house lived a chubby little girl named Sofa. A red-headed boy named Isak used to come to our yard to play.

One day Sofa took me aside and said:

"There are Jews and there are Kikes. You and me, Grisha, we're Jews. But Isak is a kike."

I was very surprised.

Frightened to Death

That same summer, immersed in Conan Doyle, I convinced myself that the Hound of the Baskervilles was circling the globe like some Wandering Jew and might at any moment pay us a visit at our dacha.

I'd wake up at night. Go into the garden wearing nothing but underpants.

Frightened to death and trembling from cold, I'd look into the darkness, awaiting the monster's shining eyes.

The Blue Hand

Along with the other boys I'd peer into the window.

The heavy blind would shift, opening a crack.

We saw a cut-off hand without skin on it.

Convinced that a human-skinning cannibal lived there, I'd run home terrified.

The "blue hand" pursued me everywhere. I raised the alarm. The grown-ups, unconcerned, failed to heed the voice crying in the wilderness.

Later, in the course of my art studies, our group was taken to the Anatomy Laboratory of the Sports Institute.

I recognized the ill-starred window.

Scaling the Wall

Another window also caught our attention. It was covered with white paint.

Scaling the wall, we looked through the transom. Washing themselves in the shower room were healthy girl athletes—discus throwers and high jumpers fresh from training at the stadium.

The girls caught us and threatened to box our ears.

We understood that to do that they would first have to dress themselves, and didn't run away too quickly.

The Blind Man

After the war, people imagined spies everywhere.

Tales were told.

For example: a spy dressed like a policeman got on a streetcar. He didn't know how much to pay for the ride. Right away the public saw through him and turned him in you know where.

Wherever you looked were cripples and invalids.

Every day at the same time, a blind man in round blue glasses appeared on our street. He slowly made his way forward, tapping his cane in front of him.

We little boys decided that he was definitely a spy. We found our friend the policeman and told him everything.

Remembering this, I still burn with shame.

Many years later, the image of a blind man appeared in my paintings.

On the Edge

My father and I went to Leningrad.

My cousin Ilya took me to the park on Vasilievsky Island to go on the Parachute Jump.

We climbed up the tower and little by little my courage deserted me. Finally we found ourselves in the clouds, on the tower's dizzying top.

Brave Ilya, not hesitating for a minute, fastened the straps, took a running jump, and disappeared.

I went out to the edge and, taking a single step, froze in place.

Those Fearsome Ballpoint Pens

It was 1957. The International Youth and Student Festival.

There were rumors that all over the city foreigners were dropping nice eye-catching ballpoint pens. A gullible Russian would fall for the bait and right away get blown to little pieces.

My parents took the children to the Riga seashore.

Away from those fearsome ballpoint pens.

Pay Heed to This

One of the methods of child-rearing in my family was the morality tale.

Mama, as if by chance, would remember a distant relative.

In his youth this relative met a young, kind, happy Russian girl by the name of Marusya. They get married and live in harmony for twenty-five years. One day he comes home and Marusya says to him out of the blue:

"Dirty Jew."

Without a word the relative takes his toothbrush and his shirt and leaves her.

At night. Forever.

The children were expected to pay heed to this.

Happy Denis

Another example.

In his youth, my father was friends with a wonderful, happy, talented fellow by the name of Denis.

Denis was full of promise. But, because of his weak character, he fell in with a bad crowd and started drinking. The hopes were dashed. Denis went on the skids.

One day the doorbell rang. At the door, his face all wrinkled, stood the legendary drunkard.

Mama gave me a meaningful look.

An Eye-Witness Report

According to Mama, in her day only prostitutes joined the Komsomol.

Too embarrassed to pronounce the dreadful word "prostitute," Mama searched for a working equivalent, for example, "a character from the movie *Nights of Cabiria*."

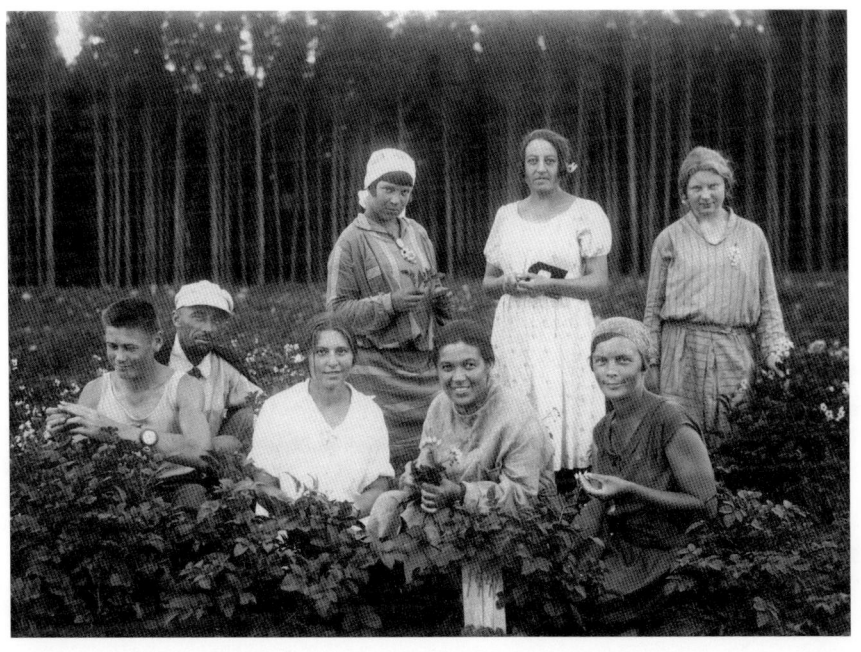

My mother is the third from the left in the first row, 1929.

The Hat

I had two great aunts, the cousins of my grandmother. They were sisters, and their names were Aunt Dora and Aunt Rachel.

One lived in Leningrad, the other in Moscow. Both of them were very old.

The sisters loved each other dearly and exchanged presents on their birthdays.

One year Dora sent Rachel a beautiful straw hat. When it was Rachel's turn to send a present she forgot the provenance of the hat and sent it back to Aunt Dora. The next year, either in revenge or out of forgetfulness, Aunt Dora returned it to her.

They kept exchanging that hat until one of them died.

How Can Anyone Believe This?

A distant relative, the tall, old Osher, shared his misgivings:

"Russians! The immaculate conception! How can anyone believe this?"

My Life's Companion

I brought my future wife Alesya to meet my great uncle and aunt.

Grandpa Iosif—in a handsome vest, with a tie on—opened the door. It seemed to him that he was insufficiently elegant. No sooner did he say hello than he disappeared, returning a minute later "comme il faut," in a good-quality jacket.

It turned out that we had mixed up the date, appearing a day early, and Grandpa had not had time to get ready.

Out came his wife, Grandma Rebecca, in a blouse with a cameo at the collar. Seeing Alesya, Grandma asked sternly, without a smile:

"Grisha, is this your life's companion?"

I affirmed it.

"Oh, what a sweetie!" she exclaimed, instantly melting.

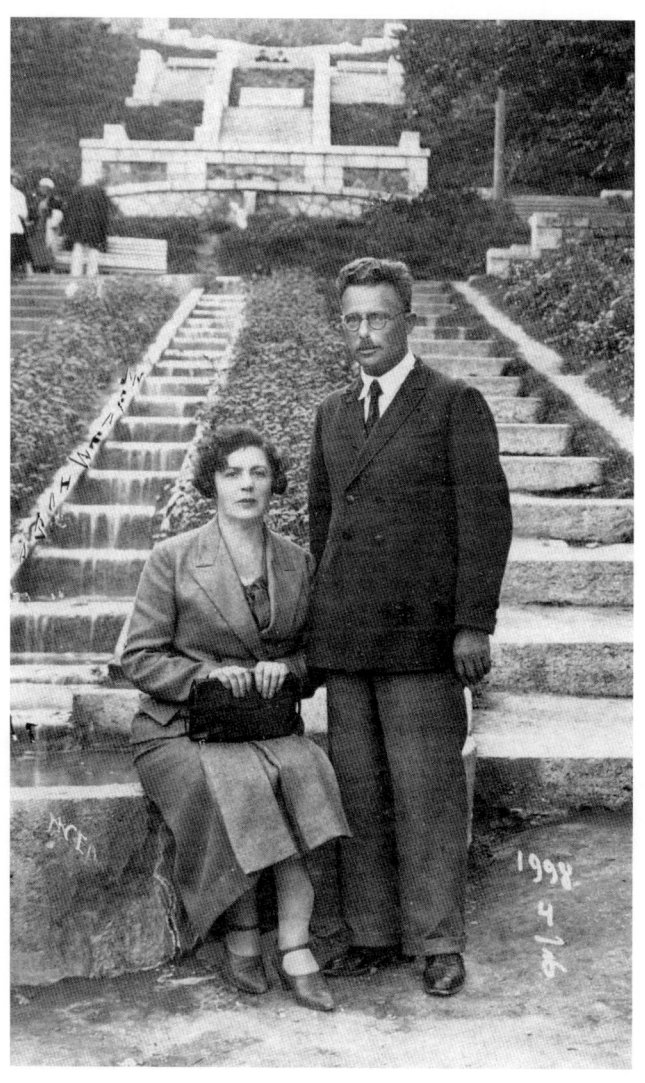

Grandpa Iosif and Grandma Rebecca.

Moonlight

A few years later, Rebecca and Iosif, who had lived out their years in love, reached the age of ninety four and decided to depart for a different world.

In the Roman fashion, by poison.

To their memory I dedicated my painting "Moonlight."

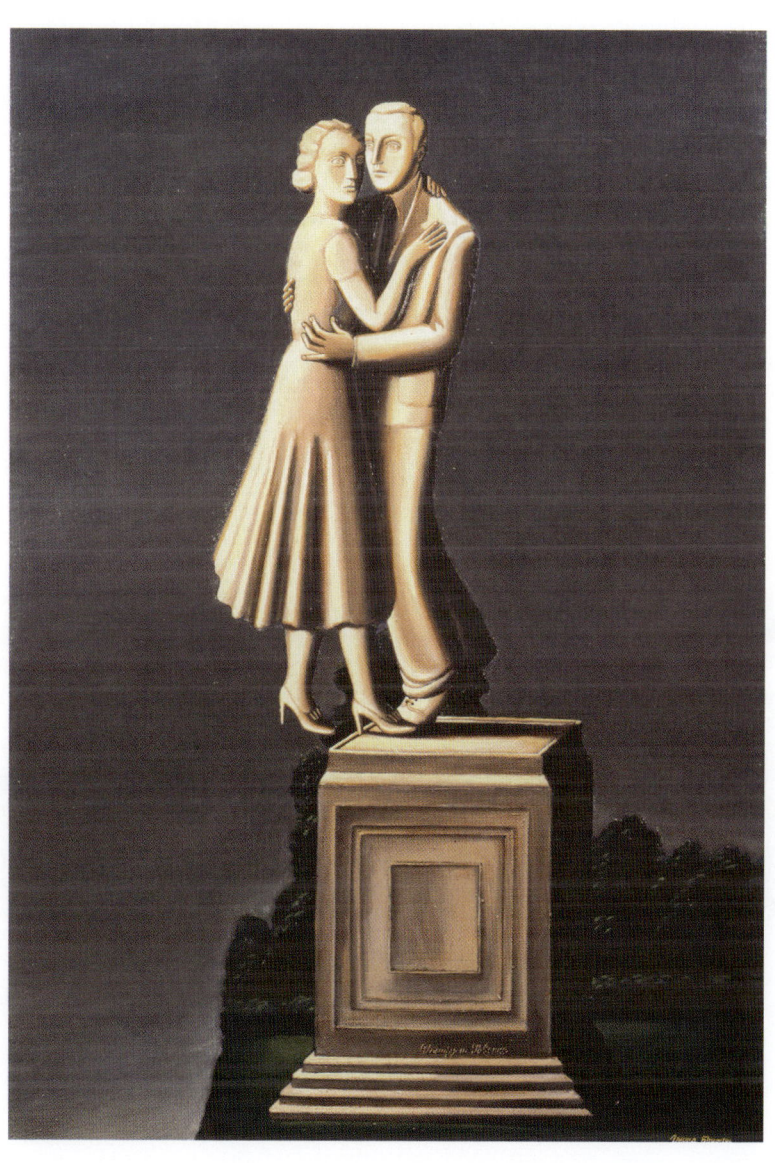

Grisha Bruskin, *Moonlight*, oil on linen.

Centralsugar

My wife, Alesya, had a set of relatives named Magaras.

All of them worked for Centralsugar:

Gidya, noted for her bad character;

Zyama, who put up with her;

Ida, whose age—a hundred and seven—never changed;

David, who suffered from constipation;

Pavlusha, who sang loud Russian folk songs in the kitchen in the hope that Ida would have a heart attack;

Pisherke Mary, the youngest;

Aleksandr, whose only amusement was reading the *Jewish Encyclopedia*;

Menya, with his Russian wife, Tanka;

Bronya, about whom nothing was known;

And finally Kisa, whom everyone looked down on because she didn't work for Centralsugar.

Once the Magarases had dug a hole in the garden, at their dacha. To save things from the Bolsheviks. But time passed and they couldn't remember where exactly it was.

"What Time Is It?"

Zyama was always asking:

"What time is it?"

"A hundred," Menya would answer.

"Plus or minus?" Zyama wouldn't miss a beat.

"No reason to make a holiday out of life," Gidya would gripe when her son Menya went to the movies.

David paid close attention to what was happening in the corridor. If someone went to the toilet, he would immediately get up and start tugging at the door.

When Pavlusha missed out on Ida's long-awaited death by dying himself, the paralyzed Ida requested that the coffin pass underneath her windows so she could be certain of her enemy's demise.

Are They Really All Alive?

Many years afterward Alesya had the following conversation with her uncle.

Alesya: "So how are the Magarases?"

Menya: "Terrific."

Alesya: "Is Ida really still alive?"

Menya: "No, Ida died a long time ago."

Alesya: "What about Bronya?"

Menya: "She died too."

Alesya: "What about David and Mary?"

Menya: "They died."

It turned out that nobody was alive.

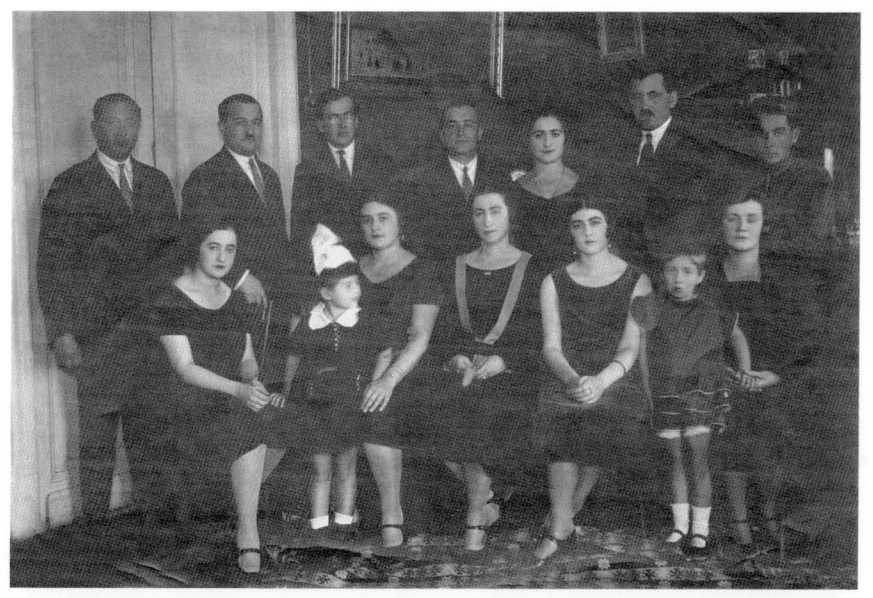

The Magaras family, with just about everyone present, Moscow, 1926.

That Old Fart Moses

Alesya also had a great uncle Moses, a collector of antiques.

In his single room were at least eighteen clocks, with cuckoos and without. It was impossible to sleep there: the clocks kept striking at different times.

Once, on the occasion of the Old Style New Year, he sent my mother-in-law a postcard with the inscription: "Dear Safochka, no Bolshevik pronouncement can change the march of nature."

He signed it: "Your old fart Moses."

When we were getting ready to emigrate to Israel, he told Alesya: "I still have something left. I'll give it to you to take along."

A Piece of Advice

When she was little, my wife, Alesya, was the special pet of a woman named Taisia Petrovna who lived in the family's communal apartment. Taisia Petrovna's husband called her "my tough babe."

Taisia Petrovna asked Alesya:

"Do they make fun of you because you're a Jew?"

"No," she said.

"Well, when they do, say, 'Jew yourself,' and even better, say 'Kike,'" advised the tough babe.

The Half-Breed

Once Alesya's brother Misha returned home from the neighbors' and solemnly declared that he, it turned out, was a half-breed.

Standing in front of the mirror, he divided his reflection first vertically and then horizontally, trying to figure out which half was breeding.

The Terrible Word

Misha came in from the street and whispered in Alesya's ear the terrible word "fluck."

Shitovna

Alesya's relative Iosif lived in Poland.

The rest of his family had perished when the Germans invaded.

Just a little boy, he was in summer camp and was saved.

Not speaking a word of Russian, Iosif roamed from place to place, hid, and finally ended up in an orphanage.

My mother-in-law found him in Moscow in the 1960s.

When it was time for his adopted daughter to get her passport, she had a tantrum, saying she was Russian and didn't want the patronymic Iosifovna.

The angry father ran from room to room and exclaimed: "She doesn't want to be Iosifovna! Shitovna, that's what she wants to be!"

In Iosif's opinion, there was no third possibility.

Creative Inspiration

I got hold of the magazine *Poland.*

Looking through it, I saw a photograph of a naked girl, taken from behind. Underneath the picture was the title "An Act of Spring."

Inspired, I quickly copied the girl.

I felt that something was clearly missing.

With the power of inspiration, the young artist-researcher penetrated deep into space and in his excitement boldly viewed the girl from the front.

Having created the second version of "An Act of Spring," I hid the album.

My older sister, Lyusya, discovered the criminal secret and threatened to tell our parents.

Her Charms Faded but Did Not Disappear

Preparing to show my work at art school, I got out "An Act of Spring."

The craftsmanship of the second version was indisputable. I couldn't decide what to do.

Finally, gritting my teeth, I took an eraser and rubbed out the girl's charms, leaving only her head.

Her charms faded, but did not disappear.

I had to use scissors.

At Dida's Birthday Party

At Dida's birthday party, I met a boy named Grisha Dorfman.

Grisha announced proudly that he went to art school. I got excited and starting asking my parents to take me there.

The school was far away, near the Moscow Planetarium.

My parents weren't up to it.

Armed with a Folder of Sketches

A few years later, armed with a folder of sketches, I set off for the Planetarium in secret from my parents.

When she saw my sketches, the director of the school, a graduate of the famous VKHUTEMAS named Natalya Viktorovna, smiled and patted my head.

I was accepted.

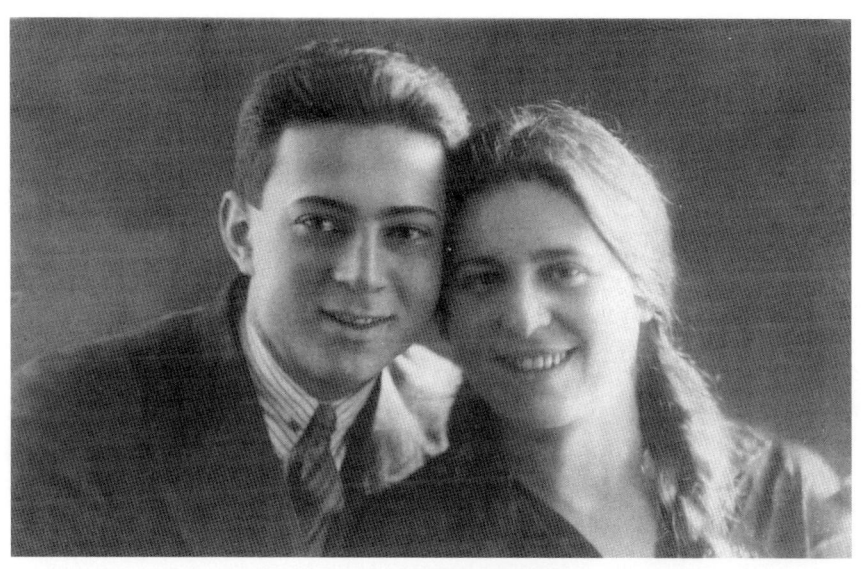

My parents, 1932.

The Freshness of Artificial Grapes

My first teacher in art school, an old man named Vladimir Ivanovich, seemed to be a devotee of the seventeenth-century Dutch school.

He gave us an assignment: reproduce in watercolors the surface of pleated silk curtains, sunlight on wineglasses filled with colored water instead of wine, the freshness of artificial grapes sprayed with water in a porcelain vase.

He retired and a new one came: Gurvich, Iosif Mikhailovich.

The newcomer was quick to correct my drawings and paintings. When he stepped away, it took work to restore them to their original state.

I remained faithful to Vladimir Ivanovich.

One day I decided to show Gurvich that if I felt like it, I could easily do what he wanted.

Iosif Mikhailovich pointed to one of the more successful parts of the new work and said:

"God grant that you always paint this way."

I believed him.

What Rina Zelyonaya and
Natalya Viktorovna Experienced

The school, housed in a fine old mansion, had a domestic feel.

I was a favorite.

When something I drew turned out well, Natalya Viktorovna, a shawl tossed over her shoulders, would walk up to me and kiss me on the forehead.

If she thought I looked sick she would call my parents and request that they feed me better.

The director was friends with the actress Rina Zelyonaya. The actress, an Order of Lenin pinned permanently to her dress, would usually come to student exhibitions.

Once I heard her say, looking at my watercolors:

"Yes, we experienced all this at the turn of the century."

I lost myself in wonder: what exactly had Rina Zelyonaya and Natalya Viktorovna experienced?

An Unreliable Profession

My father wanted me to follow in his footsteps, take up something serious, and become a Doctor of Engineering.

While he revered art, he nonetheless considered that being an artist was an unreliable profession for his son.

From childhood I wanted to do everything to counter him: I changed the pronunciation of the family name, I thought up a categorically new signature.

I couldn't stand engineering.

Deciding that things had gone too far, Father went to the art school and asked Gurvich to explain to me that I didn't have the talent to become an artist.

My teacher refused.

After Class

I was in the eighth grade of art school.

A tall girl with a clear face, around eighteen years old, was posing for us in class. The teacher drew our attention to the fact that the model was very pretty.

She gave me a friendly smile.

After class I offered to walk her home.

As we said good-bye she suddenly gave me a real kiss on the lips.

Having received the first kiss of my life, nervously excited, I returned home and ran right into the bathroom.

Until morning I didn't stop brushing my teeth and washing my mouth out with potassium permanganate. I thought that the kiss had left me with awful alien girl microbes.

I was the worthy descendant of my pharmacist grandmother.

Grisha, Do You Hear?

One evening I visited the mother of a fellow student. Her name was Galina Grigorievna, and she had been the first person in my life to give me the Bible to read.

The walls of her apartment were decorated with Russian icons and Egyptian amulets from archeological digs. Music played softly: the St. Matthew's Passion of Johann Sebastian Bach.

On the table, a four-sided Venetian lantern with stained glass made "light in the darkness."

I was invited to sit down. Each guest's face had its own color: red, green, blue, and yellow.

The hostess, bent over ancient folios, cast horoscopes for the assembled group.

Late that night, seeing me to the door, Galina Grigorievna looked past my eyes into the cosmic distance, and said slowly and clearly:

"Grisha, do you hear?"

I was embarrassed and couldn't speak. I could hear absolutely nothing, but my tongue wouldn't move to tell the truth. The psychic, who to my horror would not give up, paused for a minute, slightly widened her pupils and pronounced:

"Grisha, do you see?"

An Expressive Manner

In art school I had a friend a few years older than I was.

My friend was taking the preparatory course at the Stroganov Institute, where he sketched nudes. Once he took me along.

I was afraid I wouldn't be let in because of my age—as if it were a movie off limits to "sixteen and under."

After a satisfied inspection of my budding mustache, I did my best to dress in a mature fashion. I took a folder full of cut paper and set out for the institute.

Slipping unnoticed into the classroom, packed with legitimate grown-up fortunates, I made my way to the back row and took out my art supplies.

There was a screen in the corner. In the center of the room was an empty space with two reflectors, to keep the model warm.

With no fanfare, a totally naked rosy young woman emerged from behind the screen.

I knew that I was lost, that any second I would be found out. Blood rushed to my head like mercury in a thermometer, stopping permanently at the highest point.

Red as a tomato, in despair, I barricaded myself behind my folder. Taking an occasional, criminal glance from behind my hiding place at the "obscure object of desire" I nervously moved my soft pencil across the paper.

After a successful escape from the Stroganov Institute at the end of the session, in a semiconscious state I somehow made it home.

The next day I showed my sketches to my teacher at art school. He praised them, making particular note of my interesting expressive manner.

Crook

My friend Volodya Karp was a student at the Circus Academy.

His mother used to say:

"Yesterday you asked me for a ruble. Today you asked me for a ruble. Probably you took your friends to a restaurant. Don't be a crook like your father."

The crook father was a shoemaker.

Mama, whose relations with the Russian language were not untroubled, called the Circus Academy the Church Academy.

A Pheasant Feather

When I was in the eighth grade, my cousin Sasha Nakhimovsky came to Moscow from Leningrad.

He was older than I and struck me as a reliable man who knew everything and had experienced a lot in life.

Sasha expressed the desire to visit a Moscow restaurant, taking along some girls.

Not sure where to get them, I gave my older sister, Lera, the task of showing up with a girlfriend in the capacity of same.

In preparation for this expedition, I went to the school zoology lab, extracted a beautiful feather from a stuffed pheasant, and stuck it in a felt hat I found at home. This, I felt, was proper form for a visit to a restaurant.

We set off for a café on Kuznetsky Most, named, in the spirit of the time, Friendship.

Sasha had just come back from the genuine "West"—Vilnius— and he told us about a classy café there called Neringa, where they could and did play excellent jazz.

From that time on I longed to go to that unusual city.

Among the musicians playing at Neringa was my future friend Volodya Tarasov.

A Volume of Rilke

A few years later I realized my dream. Returning home from Vilnius to Moscow, I stopped in Leningrad.

Sasha offered to show me what Leningrad artists were doing.

That whole night we went from one studio to another. A lot of the artists didn't have telephones, so we turned up uninvited, like a bolt from the blue. Nobody was sleeping: they were working or drinking or discussing the problems of the universe. Everyone was glad to see us and happy to show their work.

When we said good-bye, Sasha gave me a volume of Rainer Maria Rilke that had just appeared. He told me to look at two excellent translations by Pasternak.

One of these poems is an interpretation of the biblical struggle of Jacob with the Angel.

Later, because of Rilke, this theme appeared in my works.

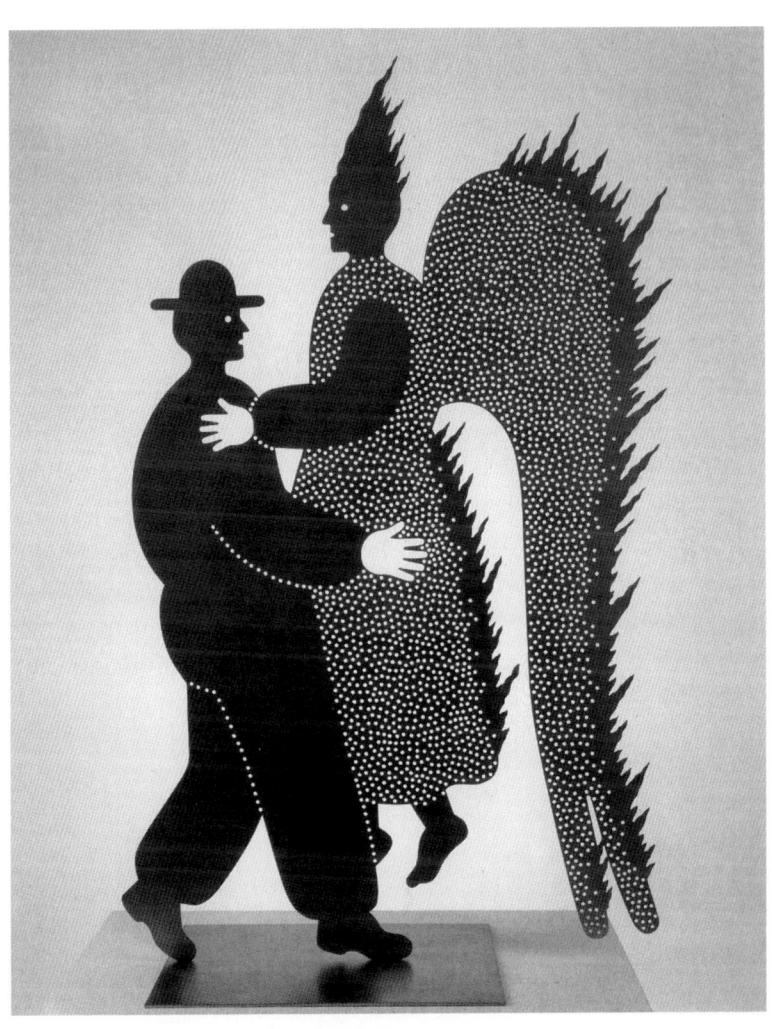

Grisha Bruskin, *Wrestling*, stainless steel.

The Son of the Vasiliev Brothers

The main purveyor of hard-to-find and forbidden literature was Sasha Vasiliev, son of one of the film-making Vasiliev brothers. It was they who had created the immortal image of Chapaev, hero of the Civil War and butt of countless jokes.

Unlike his colleagues, Sasha read everything he sold and was interesting to talk to.

Everything he earned he drank. Sometimes he appeared in the guise of a well-dressed gentleman and sometimes as a bum.

Lending out books for money was one of Sasha's businesses. The most expensive books had been published by the KGB for internal use and carried the imprint "for special distribution."

In my student years I'd pool my money with friends and give Vasiliev five rubles for a Nabokov or a Joyce.

A Lady from Back Then

I took French lessons from my dearly loved Lyolya—Elizaveta Vladimirovna Alekseeva. She was an actress, a lady from "back then," and a grand-niece of Stanislavsky.

Elizaveta Vladimirovna was incapable of talking in any language for more than five minutes. She kept switching from Russian to French, French to German, and German to English.

She lived on Nemirov-Danchenko Street.

Sometimes we went to see a relative of hers who lived in Bryusov Lane, to hear a new record by Georges Brassens or Jacques Brel. To get there we had to cross Gorky Street, and Elizaveta Vladimirovna would take a taxi.

Once in the cab, the lady "from back then" preferred communicating with the driver in French.

Every time I froze, expecting the driver to respond with something "justifiably" rude.

But some genetic impulse would overcome him. He'd start addressing Elizaveta Vladimirovna respectfully, as an aristocrat.

Zampano

Elizaveta Vladimirovna had living with her a tall, majestic-looking man with a silk scarf wrapped around his neck. This was the former actor Vladimir Karlovich Fromgold.

The first time I visited her, she told me:

"Grishenka, don't think that he's my lover. He's my butler."

The butler transcribed his thoughts about art into a thick notebook. He liked to chat with me in the kitchen, under the lampshade, about the theories of Kandinsky and Malevich.

Elizaveta Vladimirovna spoke to Vladimir Karlovich exclusively in French. Vladimir Karlovich would be annoyed.

"Lyolya, speak Russian. I don't understand."

Ignoring him, she would continue. Finally the exasperated Karlych would thunder:

"Lyolya, I'm telling you, I don't understand!"

The satisfied Lyolya drew this conclusion:

"You see, Grishenka, it's just what I've been telling you—he's a real tragic actor, a great talent, a Zampano!"

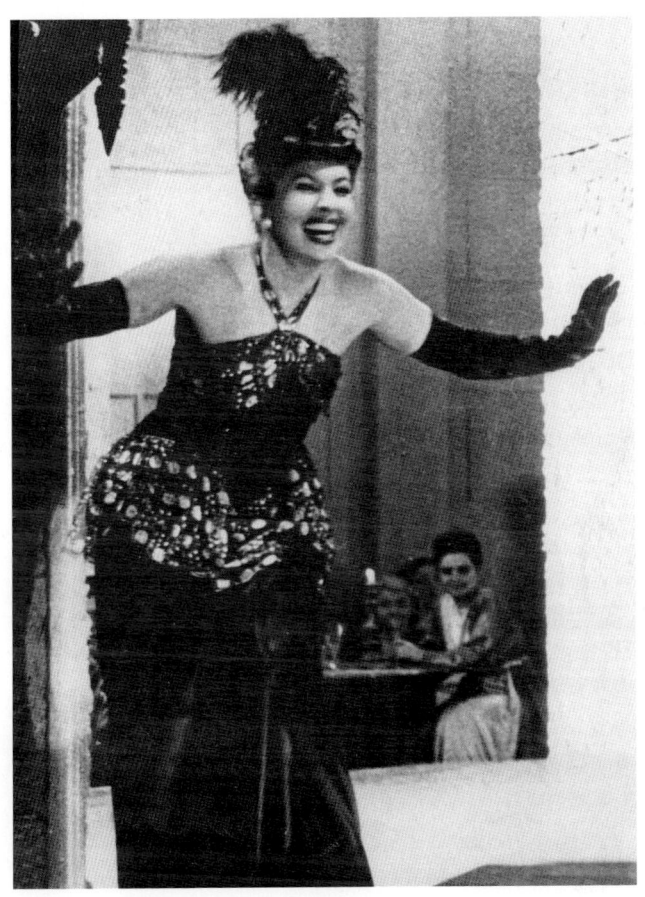

Elizaveta Vladimirovna in the role of a *chansonnière*.

A Lost World

Elizaveta Vladimirovna had a dacha in Vishnyaki.

The dacha was surrounded by Khrushchev's new housing projects. But the visitor who came up to the fence and opened the gate found himself in a lost world. Nothing even hinted that outside it was the twentieth century.

The path that led to the house went through an old, neglected lilac garden, where light rays penetrated with difficulty. In the garden were benches and sculptures.

Across the street, in a house once confiscated from the Alekseev family, resided an important Soviet general.

The state allowed Elizaveta Vladimirovna to keep her carriage house.

Lyolya took out her family album. Noble faces gazed out from the photographs.

All of them had been shot or had perished in prisons.

I Waited for This All My Life

Later, living in America, I found myself in a transatlantic lost world.

This lost world was situated on Long Island. Its mistress was the ninety-three-year-old Valentina Aleksandrovna, who had left Russia as a young girl during the Civil War.

The house was indistinguishable from a Moscow dacha. The old lady had even thought of putting a wooden outhouse in the garden.

Inside the house was Valentina Aleksandrovna's Russia: innumerable photographs of Cossack captains and the Cossack chorus in which her late husband sang; icons; portraits of the Tsar-Father.

The vacationers at this dacha were exclusively Russian.

The mistress wore shorts and drove her tenants to the railway station and to the store. The price for this service was prewar: one dollar.

When she heard that the Communist regime in Russia had collapsed, Valentina Aleksandrovna whispered through her tears:

"I waited for this all my life."

A Ticket for the Paris Metro

For a while I studied French with an old Frenchman, Monsieur Gireaux.

Twenty years earlier, the old man, annoyed with France, decided to settle in the land of the Soviets.

He never learned Russian. His circle of friends was limited to those who could speak French. Monsieur Gireaux lived in a tiny apartment way out in the middle of nowhere.

From time to time he would remove his nostalgic relics from their hiding place. Proudly he would set them on the table: a ticket for the Paris metro, a French post-office receipt, a dozen brightly colored postcards depicting Montmartre and the Cote d'Azur.

Finally, Monsieur Gireaux decided to visit his homeland to see his sister.

As soon as he got there he quarreled with her, and three days later he returned.

Existential Questions

When I started out, I lived with my parents.

I made my room into a studio. Friends would come to see me, and we'd spend entire nights discussing existential questions, with the aid of a lot of booze.

At the end of these get-togethers I would hide an impressive number of empty bottles under the bed, leaving one on the table.

In the morning, Mama would come in and express her surprise.

"Grisha, there were only seven of you and you drank a whole bottle of wine!"

A Minute More

My grandmother was a pharmacist.

Medicines were never thrown out. A whole collection was stored in a wooden kitchen cabinet

When the grown-ups went to work and my sisters to school, I, left on my own, would get out the medical treasure chest.

I was particularly attracted to vials of eye-drops. On their labels was a skull and crossbones and the intriguing inscription "Poison."

Something must have been wrong with me: pulling out the ground-glass stopper and tilting back my head, I inhaled a particular scent, unlike any other.

A minute more, and I would have been in the other world.

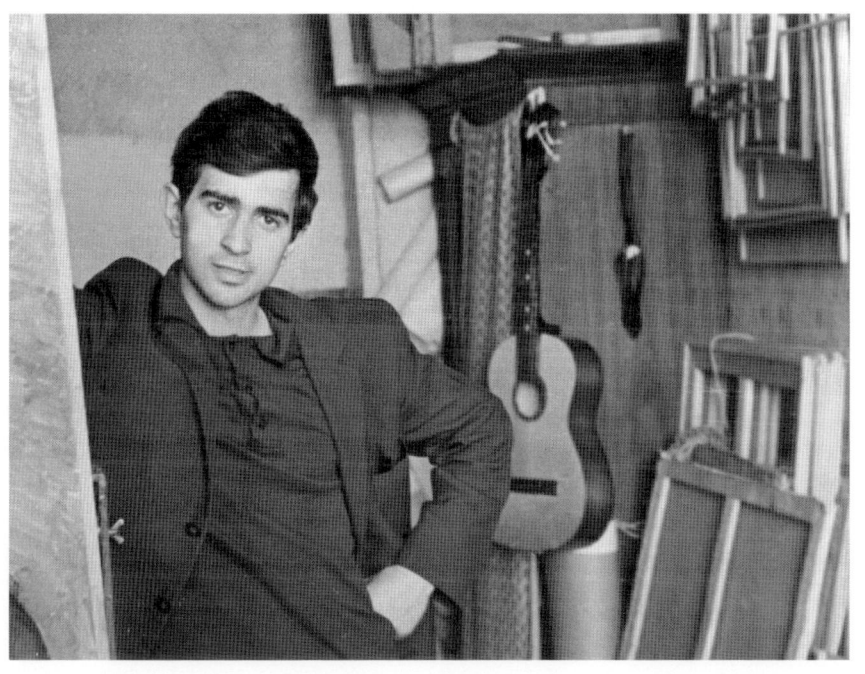

In my studio, Moscow, 1963.
Photograph by V. Savchenko.

Will I Die or Won't I?

Many years later these childish amusements came back to life .

The dentist pulled a tooth and prescribed a disgusting, bitter solution of calcium chloride.

That evening I was invited to a birthday party for my close friend, the artist Natalya Nesterova.

Since I hadn't lost my appetite I ate a lot, not neglecting to drink as well.

Arriving home at two in the morning, I remembered the loathsome calcium chloride and rummaged through the aforementioned cabinet. Pouring myself a teaspoon full, I held my nose and gulped down the medicine.

That very second I felt that I had done something irreversible. The cells, veins, and capillaries of my body were instantly paralyzed.

Looking at the vial, I discovered to my horror that I had swallowed a 40 percent solution of formaldehyde, kept at home from Grandma's prehistoric age because you never know—though I now knew.

I sat for a few seconds in a masochistic stupor, remembering alcohol-preserved frogs from my school days and two-headed fetuses from the Petersburg Kunstkamera.

Will I die or won't I?

If You Want to Live, Drink

Forcing myself to stand up, a little weak, I went to my parents' room and woke up my father.

My frightened father quickly got dressed, and a quarter of an hour later we were in the emergency room.

The doctor found out what the problem was and immediately asked:

"Did you eat anything?"

I said yes.

"Drink anything?"

I nodded (as I later found out, alcohol partially counters the effects of formaldehyde).

"Now drink," he said, putting in front of me a bucket of water.

I drank half the bucket and pleaded for mercy.

"If you want to live, drink," said the physician coolly.

My Teeth Gnashed Loudly

I wound up in intensive care, attached to an intravenous drip.

All I had gone through left me trembling all over. My teeth gnashed loudly.

To the left of me was a man who had tried to get high by drinking kerosene.

The old man to the right of me had drunk a bottle of denatured alcohol and then eaten the glass. He had had an operation to remove the pieces of glass.

The most terrifying specter was the drunk who had gorged on pesticide and turned black. He remained in the ICU forever.

I lived.

Buttons on the Fly

The Art Institute had a Military Department, which saved you from going into the army.

"War" was taught by a pockmarked colonel, who liked to use the phrase "and-no-buts."

Before the exam he said to me:

"You show up at the test in that beard—I give you an F, and-no-buts."

We were in training to become military-supply officers.

Before the exam I gleaned some interesting pieces of information from the textbook. It turned out that the trimming on a soldier's long underwear was cotton. A colonel's was rayon, and a marshal's was silk. The same system held for buttons on the fly, which were, correspondingly, plastic, bone, and mother-of-pearl.

When Was Brezhnev Born?

On a trip to Kazakhstan in my student years, I met an old *chaban* with an expressive face, by the name of Abde. I asked if I could draw his portrait.

We came to an agreement.

The *chaban*—shepherd—appeared in a straw hat, with the Order of Lenin pinned to his chest.

During the sitting, a good forty people kept their eyes on my hand. Would the portrait look like him or not?

Inspecting the result, Abde said:

"Take away the wrinkles."

I objected, explaining that the resemblance would be lost.

"You've been to the village office?" inquired the *chaban*.

Hearing an affirmative reply, he said:

"You saw Brezhnev-Kosygin? Aha. When was Brezhnev born? When was Kosygin born? And not a single wrinkle on either of them."

If Your Camel Should Drop Dead

Continuing my travels, I found myself in the village of Kulsary.

In the hotel I was struck by a notice:

"Citizens! The plague is a dangerous illness . . ."

Walking into the cafeteria, I saw another one:

"If your camel should drop dead for no apparent reason . . ."

A little concerned, I asked why the masses were being warned about a medieval disease.

It turned out that a quarantine for the plague had just been lifted.

A Fistful of Coins

In the hotel an excited concierge ran up to me and said that a flying scorpion was in the building, threatening everyone with a fatal bite.

My roommate turned out to be a "mean Chechen," who, "sharpening his dagger," had killed his neighbor in blood revenge.

I decided it was time to go. I gathered my belongings. Got on a bus.

A man got on behind me. Mumbling something, he stuck his hand in his mouth, pulled out a fistful of coins and paid for the ride.

I flew out on the street like a shot.

The Hiding Place

I was sitting in a teahouse, in the shadow of a plane tree, in the city of Urgut, Uzbekistan. I was drinking green tea and anticipating the arrival of pilaf.

Mountains surrounded me. A gurgling river flowed nearby. A slogan over the teahouse sparkled in the sun: "May the name Vladimir Ilyich Live into Eternity."

I got to talking with the man sitting next to me at the table. Learning that I was from "Moscow itself," my neighbor, Abdurazak Tursunovich, refused to let me pay for the food and invited me to visit him at work, in the Party's district bureau. Out of curiosity I agreed.

In Abdurazak Tursunovich's office, next to his chair, loomed an enormous plaster bust of Lenin.

Without saying a word, the hospitable host lifted the hollow bust and extracted from its hiding place a bottle of Stolichnaya.

After the vodka, I recklessly told him my Moscow phone number.

With a Dazzling Flash of Gold Teeth

Soon afterward, the phone rang in my apartment.

Abdurazak informed me that he was in the capital together with two comrades. They were on their way to Bulgaria and wanted to give me a melon.

I invited the guests to the Metropol restaurant.

The comrades turned out to be two Uzbek women, outfitted for a trip abroad in knit dresses under which you could see their colorful national pants. Both of them were named Gulsara.

With a dazzling flash of gold teeth, the girls smiled and started eating.

After the soup, one Gulsara fell asleep; the other turned on a Spidola transistor radio she had brought with her.

The Death of Two Comrades

Ten days later, on the return trip, Abdurazak Tursunovich appeared in my apartment.

"Where are the comrades?" I inquired.

"They are dead to me," he snapped.

It turned out that once abroad, the comrades had absconded and sold the Spidola.

A Kebab Tool

The director of a school in Urgut invited me home.

On the way he asked:

"Why are you so thin? Are you poor or are you sick?"

A shepherd drove his flock across the road. Pointing his finger at a sheep that had stayed behind, the teacher pronounced:

"A kebab tool."

On Carpets

We arrived at his house.

The women brought in an abundance of food and drink. The men reclined on carpets surrounded by pillows.

There was a toast to the eternal friendship of Russians and Uzbeks. Glass after glass was downed.

Having stuffed themselves to within an inch of their lives, the company stretched out on the same carpets and went to sleep.

A Witches' Brew

In the morning, the school director winked and informed us that in his barn he was drying opium poppies and hemp. And that the time had come to taste the fruit thereof.

He tossed into transparent green tea bits of a substance resembling tar. The liquid instantly turned thick and black: a witches' brew.

A World of Colors Never Before Seen

The elixir worked its magic. Host and guests had clearly set off for the world of illusions.

I prepared to join them.

Nothing happened. The journey did not take place.

Disappointed, I set off for the bus station.

Halfway There

Halfway there I started feeling sick.

I lost consciousness. Woke up in a ditch at the side of the road. And that was the end of that.

The shepherd of schoolboys had failed to awaken me to the magical hemp-and-opium kingdom.

I Want to Be in Moscow!

My Uzbek travels over, I took a taxi to the airport.

Riding with me were two Muscovites, both good-looking young women. One of them asked the driver to stop the car and went out for glass of seltzer.

The driver turned to the remaining girl.

"Where are you from, sister?"

"Moscow."

"Moscow itself?"

"Yes."

"Married?"

"Yes."

"Children?"

"Yes."

"Is your girlfriend also from Moscow?"

"Yes"

"Married?"

"Yes."

"Children?"

"Yes."

"I want to be in Moscow," concluded the driver dreamily, clicking his tongue.

Perfection Has No Limit

At age twenty-three, on the strength of my juvenilia, I entered the Artists Union.

I was invited to join an artists' group on a trip to the Russian North.

In the group was a pretty girl named Tanya G., who painted northern landscapes with a heavy academic hand. She was accompanied by her admirer Feinstein, a tall journalist of advancing years.

No matter where we turned up, the local papers would run a story, signed by someone named Dymov. The story would begin more or less as follows:

"A bright new morning. Silence. A light wind ruffles the mirrored surface of the lake. A seagull dips its wing. In the distance echoes a ship's horn.

"What beauty! An artist should behold it, a real one.

"And here they are, magicians and sorcerers!"

The story would conclude:

"Back from her sketching, indomitable and always dissatisfied with herself, Tanya G. spent even more time casting her magic spells over her canvas. Because she wants to make a masterpiece. In truth, perfection has no limit."

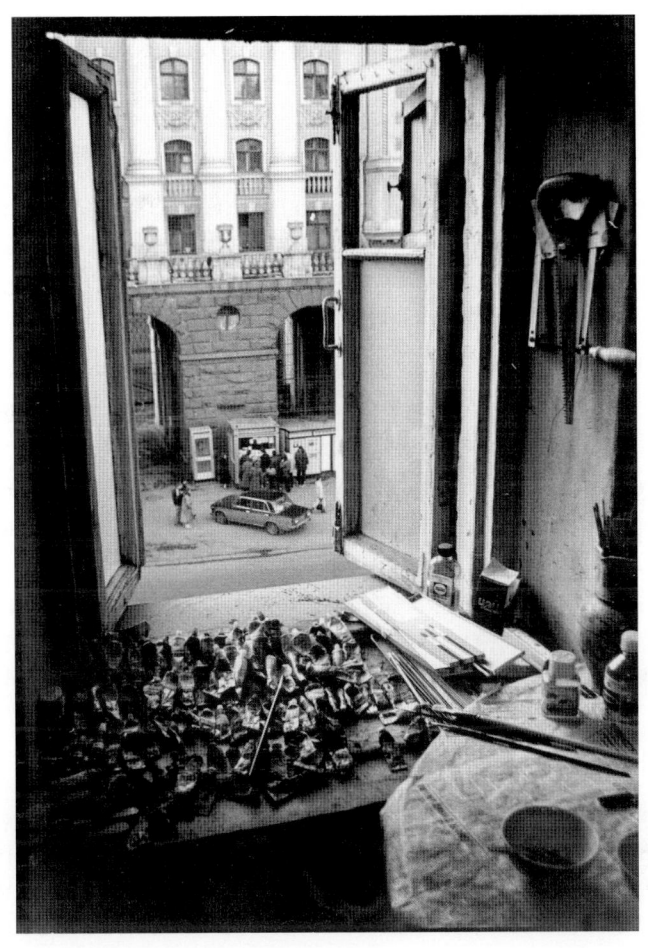

Window. My studio on Mayakovsky Square, 1986.

Being a Gypsy in Holy Russia

One time the artists were taken on a bus tour.

From the windows of the bus appeared a gypsy tent, set up in a field.

On a trunk in front of the tent was a steaming samovar. A dark gypsy with pitch-black hair and beard was sitting and drinking tea. Beside him was a guitar. From behind him gazed his lovely blue-eyed wife. Two agile daughters busied themselves with the housekeeping. A horse, a dog, and a cat completed the picture.

Imagining myself in a Pushkin poem, I asked the driver to stop the bus and got out.

Seeing me, the gypsies starting waving their hands, beckoning me to join them, which I did.

The affable host offered me vodka. He said that they were on vacation and "stripping bark" to sell. With my beard and long hair, I looked a bit like a gypsy, which my new friends affirmed.

When we finished the bottle, we set off for the village to get another.

No sooner had the "two gypsies" turned up in the little village than the local boys started throwing stones at us. Curses, damnations, and insults rained down on us from every courtyard.

Barely alive, we made it to the grocery.

I understood that being a gypsy in Holy Russia was no picnic.

Strange People

Some friends and I were on vacation in the Ukraine.

In the evening we came to the little village Ovruch.

In the twilight I noticed strange people in prehistoric clothes. It seemed to me that I knew them.

Looking more closely, I suddenly understood that they were all Jews. Saved by some miracle from the Nazis.

I thought:

"Maybe they still have their old books."

You Wouldn't Understand This

A few days later I found myself back in Ovruch.

I went into a rickety old shoe store. On the shelves were heaps of shiny black galoshes with red linings.

Behind the counter was an old Jew in a hat and jacket, shooting the breeze with a Ukrainian peasant woman.

I said hello and asked if he could sell me a Talmud.

Figuring this was a provocation, the salesman stood up straight and said in a loud voice:

"I fought in the war and was awarded the Order of the Red Star."

From which I understood that, apparently, he did not have a Talmud.

The uncomprehending peasant woman asked what we were talking about.

"Oh! You wouldn't understand!" exclaimed the veteran in a heavy Jewish accent.

The Poems of a New Friend

In 1965, I met the artist Misha Odnoralovy.
My new friend came to see me in my studio and said:
"I just wrote some poems. Here, let me recite them."
He recited some poems by Mandelstam, which I knew by heart.

Don't Mess with Our Russian Art

Once Misha painted a still life with icons.

At a drunken party, the artist Ksyusha Nechitailo came up to him and, being a straight-talker, told him the unvarnished truth:

"You, Misha, stop messing with our Russian art. Look at Grisha, he doesn't mess with it, and good for him."

An Israeli Army Officer

Misha went to America and found happiness with a nice Israeli Army officer named Chaya.

At some point the fortyish Chaya started to put on weight. She went on a diet and got thinner, but then she started gaining weight again. Nothing helped.

One day on the street Chaya ran into an old Israeli friend and started complaining.

"Chaya," he said, "you're crazy, you're just pregnant."

According to the doctor, in the sixth month.

Officer Chaya presented the graying Misha with a charming son, Andryusha.

St. George the Dragon Slayer

Traveling in the Russian Far North, my friend and I came across a wonderful old lady with a face full of freckles.

She had whiled away her life in this village forgotten by man and God, surrounded by the real, no-nonsense taiga and wolves.

In her hut, in the icon corner, hung a portrait of Marshal Voroshilov on a white horse, cut out of *Ogonyok* magazine.

The old lady crossed herself and knelt before Voroshilov, thinking that he was St. George the Dragon Slayer.

A Set of Male Attributes

Her favorite diversion was a game she played with an orange cat.

Hiding with a bucket full of water, Grandma would delight in splashing the contents over the unfortunate animal's head.

Her second favorite was making marvelous toy figures out of clay, among which her best-loved was Polkan, a centaur.

While she was working the sculptress would suddenly blush and start giggling enigmatically. Then, turning away, she would skillfully supply the mythological creature with a set of male attributes.

A Devil with Tail and Horns

We spent a few days with the old lady and her cat, doing our best to help out with the housework and supply her with food.

She doted on us.

When we parted, she told me:

"It's good, Grigory Ivanovich, that you have visited us and not some kind of Jew."

From Grandma's far-away, Jews were devils with tails and horns.

Man in a Hat

In 1973, using my privileges as a member of the Artists Union, I went to Gurzuf on a creative retreat.

The group leader was my good friend Lyosha Sokolov. Among the participants was the artist Vitya Popkov, who was very popular at the time.

Once, strolling around the resort town, I went into the Summer Breeze café. There was Vitya, sitting in the Summer Breeze and drinking.

Vitya was going through a painful spell and wanted to talk. He invited me to join him.

We discussed Vitya's life, together with global problems, and, quite smashed, went outside for some fresh air.

Popkov needed to piss, which he did off to the side.

Up came a man in a hat and asked him not to make a disturbance in a public place. Vitya sent him packing.

Forgetting about the socially minded citizen, we went home. But he did not forget about us.

And ratted.

A Straitjacket

Suddenly our path was blocked by a police jeep.

From which emerged four big guys who started tying us up.

We resisted a little and then gave in.

At the police station, Vitya informed the cops that history would not forgive them the arrest of two geniuses, and that if the Vietnam War were raging now, it would be us, and not them, who would fight as volunteers with the heroic Vietnamese people, marching with gun in hand against the American aggressor.

They put Popkov in a straitjacket and carted us off to the Yalta Drunk Pen.

As a Sign of Protest

In the Drunk Pen they stripped us down to our underwear, took away our IDs, and put us in the hands of a rigorous Medical Commission.

Vacillating between narcotics and drunkenness, the Commission issued its verdict: severe alcoholic intoxication.

In disagreement with the opinion of this forum and as a sign of protest, Vitya tore off his underwear and threw it in the face of the offenders.

They shoved us into a cell and locked the heavy metal door. Looking around, we saw a full chamber pot, bars on the windows, and a row of cots covered with oil cloth and riveted to the floor for security.

On one of the cots sprawled a man, semiconscious.

When we woke him up, the alcoholic informed us that he didn't remember how long he had been there and had no idea when he would get out.

In the morning they gave us our clothes, but not before making us carry out the loathsome chamber pot.

Telling us that we'd get our IDs at the police station on Monday, they liberated us.

Freed at last and seated in a taxi, we drove cheerfully through the flowering springtime Crimea back home to Gurzuf.

Wisely Providing a Circumcision

Back in Gurzuf, Polkov felt an unprecedented surge of creative inspiration.

He got to work immediately. Made a frame, stretched a canvas of three meters by two.

Continuing his nonstop drinking, Vitya worked indefatigably on his painting entitled "Artists in the Drunk Tank," trying from time to time to get me to help him.

On Sunday toward the end of the day the masterpiece was ready.

The painting showed two Promethean artists at the moment of a Drunk Tank inspection.

Vitya had not forgotten to retrieve his own underwear, but he left me without mine, wisely providing a circumcision.

Comrade Officer, Have Mercy

Monday morning we went to the police station to get our passports.

The officer in charge informed us that we were being charged with violation of the criminal code, article two (particularly aggravating conduct) for insulting a law enforcement agent and resisting arrest. And that we were to go from the police station directly to court.

Soon after, we were marched to the court building through the entire town, under police escort. Our path crossed the Summer Breeze café.

As we approached this dive, Vitya felt the urge to sign in. He turned to the guard.

"Comrade Officer, have mercy. My throat is dry. Let me get a glass of water."

The policeman agreed, and Vitya instantly disappeared into the Summer Breeze.

Horror-struck, I hastily got the cop's okay and chased after him.

It was too late. Vitya had already polished off a glass of vodka and was following it with a pickle.

Sentence

The judge issued an exceptionally light sentence, a monetary fine and expulsion from the southern shore of the Crimea. A record of the proceedings would be sent to our place of work (the Artists Union) along with a caricature depicting the drunken artists in a green vodka bottle.

It turned out that the judge was a good friend of our group leader Lyosha Sokolov. Before the trial, Lyosha selflessly had a drink with him, pleading with him not to transfer the case from civil to criminal court.

The judge agreed out of friendship, exacting a crate of cognac to seal the deal.

We were saved.

Point-Blank

Soon after, in Moscow, on Gorky Street, at nine o'clock in the evening Vitya was trying to catch a cab to take him home.

A cash courier stopped for him.

The drunk courier rolled down his window, aimed his pistol straight at Vitya's throat and shot him point-blank, killing the artist instantly.

Give Some Thought to This

The first works that I consider my own belong to the end of the 1960s, right after my graduation from the institute.

Toward 1975, I had accumulated enough paintings for an exhibition.

The exhibition, set up for a single evening under the auspices of the Painters Club, was to be held at the House of Art on Kuznetsky Most. The organizer of this event, my friend Zhora Satel, was an artist no longer young and a member of the club's governing board.

The exhibition was intended for art professionals. Entrance was by invitation, and tickets were distributed in accordance with a list the board had approved.

Responsibility for this was given to Lyubov Semyonovna Rabinovich, an elderly Communist artist.

I wrote out the names of the people I wanted to see.

The night before the event, Rabinovich, dressed in the military style of the early 1920s, with a map bag on a strap, handed me the approved guest list.

To my astonishment I saw that all the Jewish names had been crossed off in Lyubov's own neat hand.

Trying to understand what this might mean, I asked her for an explanation.

Drawing close, Lyubov Semyonovna looked me straight in the eye, as if peering into the imminent bright future and, in a loud whisper that invited me into the conspiracy, said:

"You and I, Grisha, should give some thought to this as well."

Go Fuck . . .

The exhibition had to be approved by the Party.

In the course of the day, the Party approved and prohibited it several times. Finally, at four o'clock, under pressure from Zhora Satel, the officials caved in and granted permission.

Later Zhora told me that when he returned home to have a bite to eat and change before the opening, he started off with a shot of vodka.

In an emotional state, alone in the room, he decided to make a toast. Surprising himself, he said:

"Grisha's luck . . . My luck . . . Go fuck . . ."

A Worker with Golden Hands

In the 1970s, at the Moscow Artists Union building on Begovaya Street, I ran into the artist Vitaly Komar. He had a painting under his arm.

"I want to join the Artists Union," declared Vitaly. "So I made a special trip to the Hammer and Sickle factory to paint the portrait of the old worker Ivanov. I called the painting 'A Worker with Golden Hands.' But just now for some reason they turned me down. Want to have a look?"

Komar revealed a carefully drawn, realistic portrait of a man marked by a life of honest labor.

The worker's hands were neatly covered with thick golden paint.

Wives Come and Go

I had a friend, Mikhail Semyonovich Matskovsky. He was a well-known sociologist who studied marriage and the family.

The sociologist's private life was a complete disaster: one hopeless wife after another.

Studying this situation, he arrived at a scholarly conclusion: "Wives come and go, but friends remain."

Down with Marriage!
Up with the Life of a Wild Wolf!

Matskovsky was giving a birthday party.

I had just split with my first wife and as a result of this was in a state of heavenly euphoria, basking in bachelorhood.

Declaring "Down with marriage! Up with the life of a wild wolf!", I went to my friend's place.

Right away, my eyes lit on a beautiful, graceful girl, my future wife, Alesya.

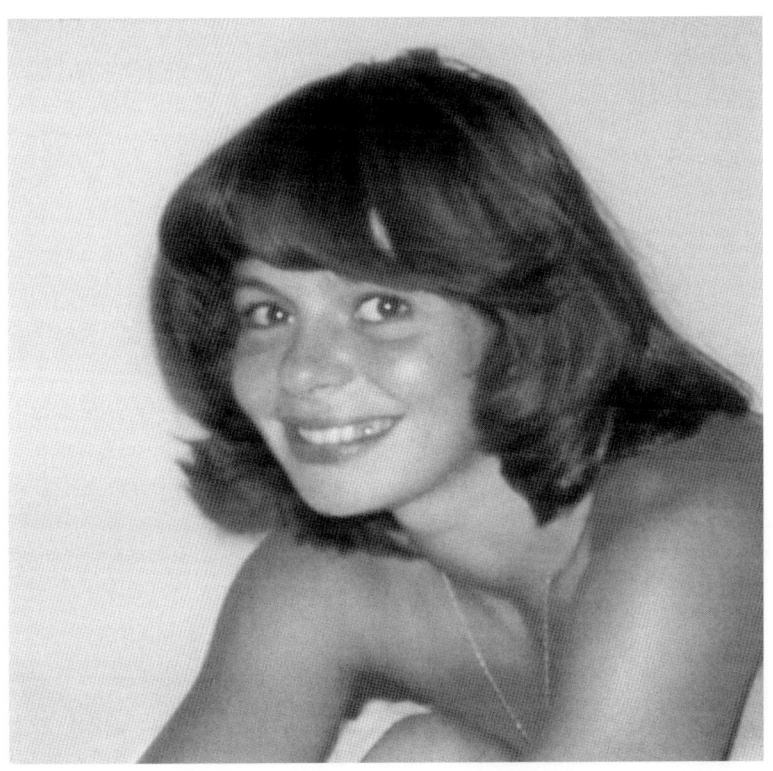

Alesya.

In the Language of Stendhal

Celebrating my first month of long-awaited freedom, I spent a lot of time smashed.

When my friend's latest companion informed me that the object of my interest knew French, I boldly decided to court her in the language of Stendhal.

For her part, Alesya had a drunken-artist father, and she felt no desire to make friends either with artists or alcoholics.

Nevertheless, by the end of the evening I had managed to obtain the desired telephone number.

Mikhail Semyonovich asked that his gravestone be engraved with the following epitaph:

"Here lies the man who introduced Grisha to Alesya."

An Amazing Combination of Red and Gold

Alesya's father, Yury Georgievich, was a book illustrator.

As befits a pupil of Isaac Brodsky, he worked in a realistic style.

All his heroes were blue-eyed blonds; villains were brunettes with thin mustaches and checkered jackets.

Alesya's father divided his time between work and drink.

Once, drunk, Yury Georgievich got on a bus and ended up near Kalinin.

My mother-in-law got a telegram:

"Dear Safochka! There's an amazing combination of red and gold here. Send three to five rubles."

Strange but True

My father-in-law was summoned by the Party.

The section head told him that the Party had made the wise decision to publish the *Short Course on the History of the Party* for young people, and proposed to the artist that he illustrate it.

Yury Georgievich detested Soviet power. Seeking a plausible excuse, he said:

"All my life I have been illustrating science fiction: Kazantsev, the Strugatsky brothers . . . "

"Then you know the ropes," retorted the section head.

Coffee and Tea

From my mother-in-law Safo Vladimirovna I found out that "with acquaintances you drink coffee, with girlfriends you drink tea."

Asya Fyodorovna and Her Boundless Possibilities

Yury Georgievich was friends with one of his neighbors in the communal apartment, a theatrical master-of-ceremonies by the name of Glebochka.

When he got home, the master-of-ceremonies would greet everyone in his accustomed manner:

"Hello, Good evening!"

Glebochka's wife, Asya Fedorovna, was a big shot—a theater director at Russconcert. The stars of Soviet variety shows came to pay their respects to her.

Glebochka would say:

"Asya Fyodorovna and her accessibility. Asya Fyodorovna and her utility. Asya Fyodorovna and her boundless possibilities."

When payday came around, "her boundless possibilities" would send Glebochka to the far reaches of the vast Motherland. She was afraid that her alcohol-prone husband would squander the family money.

Chippolino Is a Sick Old Lady

Moonlighting at children's New Year celebration, Glebochka dressed up as the old man Khottabych and took the five-year-old Alesya to a matinee.

At intermission Khottabych took the little girl backstage.

Her mouth agape, the enchanted Alesya watched as theatrical mysteries revealed themselves before her.

When the bell rang for the beginning of the second act, the assistant director yelled:

"Pinocchio, onstage!"

To which Pinocchio—played by a young actress—responded:

"They keep using me to fill in holes. It's Chippolino's entrance."

The director reproached Pinocchio:

"You ought to be ashamed of yourself. Chippolino is a sick old lady. They just had to give her a shot!"

A Woman Must Remain a Mystery

Seeing that Alesya was about to go out, Asya Fyodorovna asked her:

"Where are you going, honeybunch?"

"To the beach with my friends."

"Boys too?" her voice got tense.

"Boys too."

"Honeybunch, this is out of the question," exclaimed Asya Fyodorovna. "People get undressed at the beach! And a woman must remain a mystery."

Asya Fyodorovna herself, in her desire to remain a mystery to her husband Glebochka, would dress and undress in the hallway of the communal apartment.

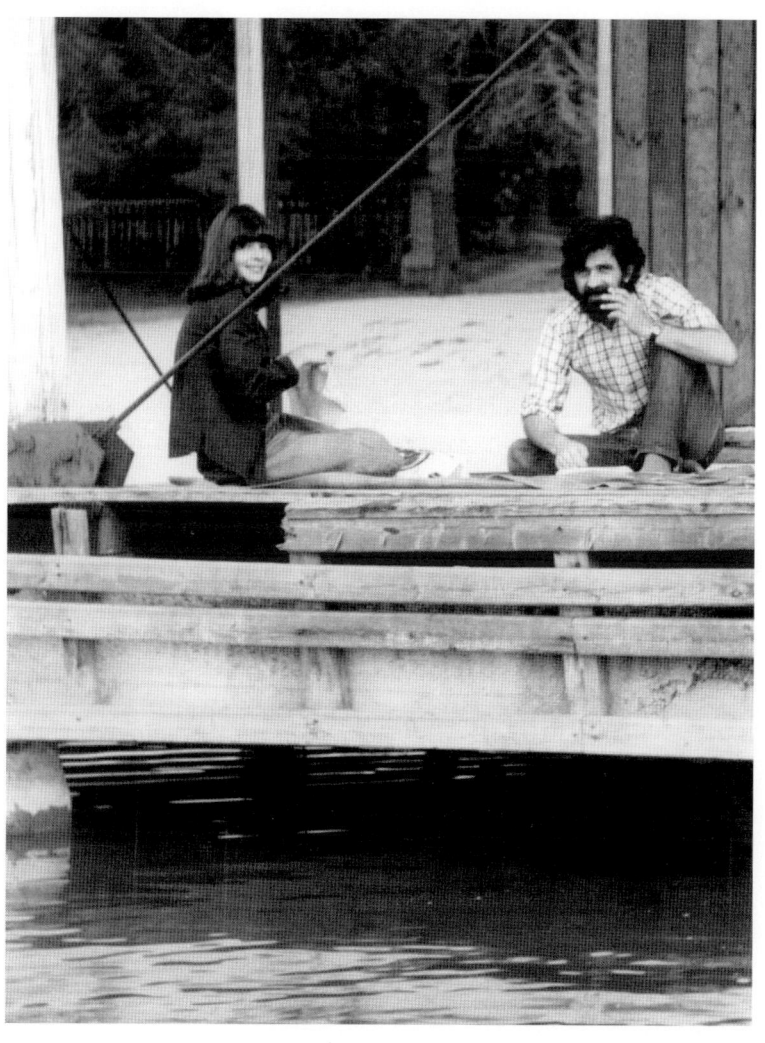

With Alesya, Elva, 1982.

The Curse

Glebochka's first wife was a provincial singer named Lyuba.

At the height of her powers Lyuba suddenly fell ill and died.

Before her death, in a state of serious depression, she took an unconscionable step: she cursed her husband and her ten-year-old daughter Yulya.

Events unfolded as follows:

Yulya, a blue-eyed girl with flaxen hair, was returning home from final exams.

There was an accident on the road. Two cars hit each other. The carburetor of one of the cars flew out and hit the girl in the legs. She fell. She broke her spine and a week later she was dead.

Glebochka was inconsolable.

One day his new wife, Asya Fyodorovna, was at the stove making face cream. She was wearing a nylon robe. The robe caught fire. Asya Fyodorovna went up in flames.

In his grief, the widower started drinking.

He got married again. He had a son, Sashka.

A few years later Glebochka unexpectedly hanged himself.

Moms!

My mother-in-law had a friend from the university, Serafima Moiseevna. She was an invalid and lived alone until she adopted the orphan Valentin.

The grateful Valentin grew fond of Serafima Moiseevna and called her "Moms."

The guy liked to ask:

"Moms! Hey, Moms! When we start beating up Jews, Moms, will we beat you up too?"

Hey, Pumpkin, What a Big Boy You Are!

Our Aunt Adulya spoke an earthy kind of Russian.

We never invited her home, hoping to spare the ears of our well-brought-up son, Tyoma.

When Tyoma had his tenth birthday, my mother-in-law decided, finally, to invite Adulya to the celebration.

Standing at the door, the guest caught sight of the birthday boy and screeched in delight:

"Hey Pumpkin! Shit, what a big boy you are! Got a broad yet?"

We're Taking the Bank

The artist Volodya Yankilevsky had a broken gun he had been using in an assemblage. He didn't need it any more, so he threw it into the garbage.

His neighbor, my friend Igor Kozlov, was walking his dog when he saw the gun and picked it up.

At that time, our mutual friend Misha Matskovsky had left his most recent wife and taken up residence with Igor.

When he arrived home with his find, Igor started fooling around.

"So, Mish, here's the gun. We're taking the bank, the telegraph, the post office, the radio station. You'll be my cover," and so on.

Perhaps for the Last Time

The next day, the innocent Misha—Mikhail Semyonovich—went to work.

He was sent to Security.

There he was met by a square-jawed man who politely motioned him over to a black Volga. Accompanied by some "comrades," he was taken to Petrovka 38: Criminal Investigation.

Uncomprehending, my friend sadly, perhaps for the last time, looked through the car window at the spring landscape and the majestic silhouette of Moscow University.

When the car passed Red Square, a thought passed his mind: "I never got to Lenin's Mausoleum."

In a Criminal Lineup

When they arrived at Petrovka House, the first thing Misha heard was the voice of the guard, reporting by internal telephone:

"They've brought Matskovsky."

The investigator spent a few minutes talking with Misha on general topics. Then he put a handful of photographs on the desk.

Monsters of all sizes and shapes stared at him from the snapshots. Suddenly in the criminal lineup he caught sight of his best friend Igor Kozlov.

At that very moment in the next room, the same thing was happening to Igor.

Igor Kozlov was married to an Englishwoman. His telephone was bugged.

Hearing his criminal plans, the KGB operatives had taken measures.

How Wonderful This Is!

We had a friend, Jean-Michel, a nice French mathematician.

A dyed-in-the-wool leftist, he liked everything he saw in the Soviet Union.

The young man went into ecstasy when a waiter in a restaurant refused to serve him for an entire hour and when he finally came over spoke rudely.

"How wonderful this is!" said the Frenchman. "People in this country aren't afraid of losing their jobs."

An Exciting Political Demonstration

On one of his visits to Russia, our friend stayed with Alesya's brother in an apartment a floor below ours.

At six in the morning there was a knock on the door. We opened up to find an excited Jean-Michel.

"You're lying here asleep and telling everybody that there's no freedom or democracy in this country. But I was up all night watching a political demonstration. People were lighting bonfires, shouting things into a megaphone. Police were everywhere!"

On the ground floor of our building was a big department store. The exciting political demonstration was a queue for carpets. People wrote numbers on their hands, and these numbers were then called out by megaphone.

It's true that there were bonfires. And police.

The Love of a Russian Girl

Finally, Jean-Michel fell for the passionate love of a Russian girl and got married.

After struggling together to get her to the West, the young couple was reunited at the Roissy airport.

The girl asked for a separate taxi.

Jean-Michel never saw her again.

The Historical Argument of Two Nations

In the city of Brest I went to the train station toilet.

And spent at least a couple of hours there, engrossed in the graffiti.

Immigrating Jews, leaving their country forever, formulated on the walls of this secluded space some choice thoughts about Russians and Russia.

The local population instantly counterattacked, pouring out everything that had been pent up in their souls. The next immigrants provided commentary on these texts, provoking the continuation of the dialogue. And so on.

Finally someone dipped a brush into a pail of green paint and wrote above it all in huge bold letters, "Jew Motherfuckers," as though summing up the historical argument of two great nations.

They Shook Hands on It

In 1977, my friend Edik Lozansky decided to forsake the shores of his fatherland and move to America.

His father-in-law was at that time the commander of the Kiev Military District. Under his command, in 1968, Soviet troops had marched into Prague.

Edik's father-in-law asked the couple to get a divorce and wait a few months, until he received his promotion and its next new star. After this, the war plan had Edik's wife, Tanya, reuniting with her husband.

They shook hands on it. Edik emigrated. The general really did get his promotion, becoming General Commander of Civil Defense of the USSR. Stroking his new epaulettes, he moved to Moscow.

He called for Tanya and told her he would never let her go. He told her to forget her husband, and that he had his eye on a nice young major for her.

Tanya, like a true general's daughter, gave a categorical "no" and, showing her iron will, began a struggle to reunite the family.

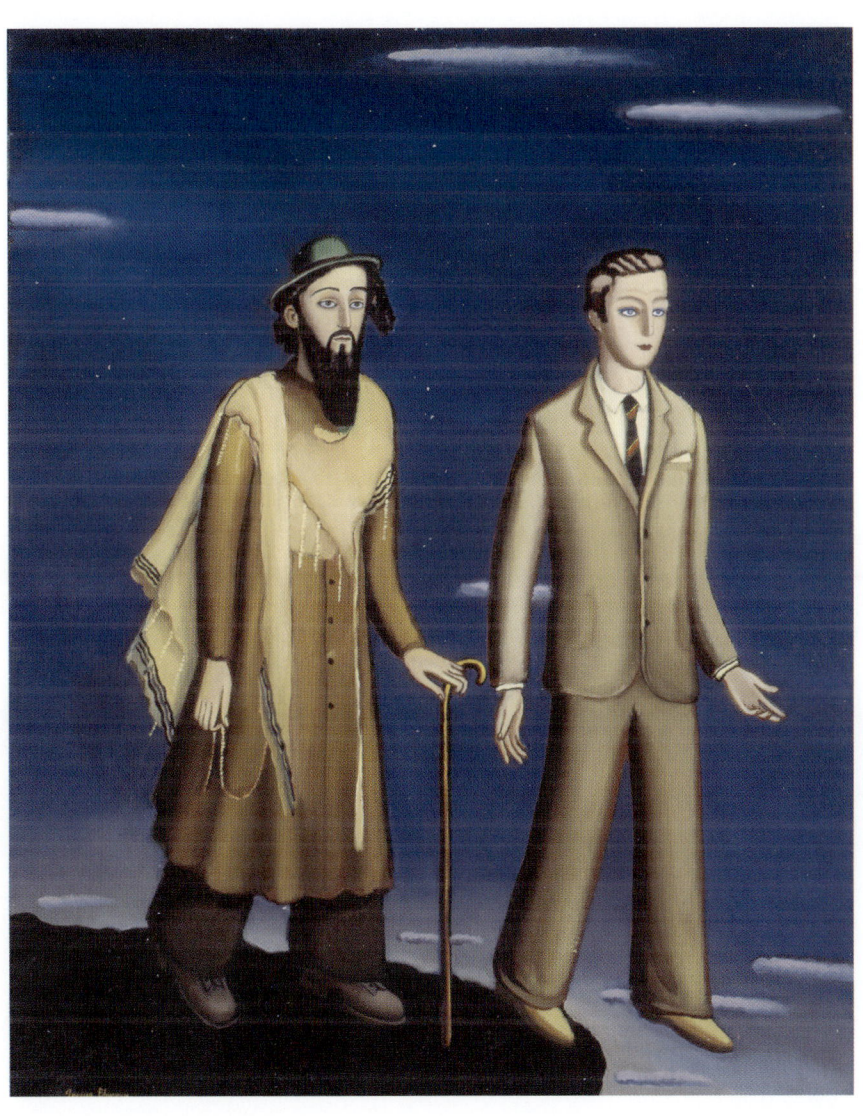

Grisha Bruskin, *The Partner,* oil on linen.

A Dangerous, Covert Enemy

Feeling responsible for my friend and empathizing with Tanya, I tried to give her help and moral support to the best of my strength and abilities.

One day Tanya came to see me in my studio. She said her father had seemed to be strikingly knowledgeable about all her friends. He informed her that the most harmful among them was an artist whose studio was on Mayakovsky Square.

"This is a dangerous, covert enemy," concluded the general. "We'll deal with him soon."

The commander's best friend was Fedorchuk, the then head of the KGB.

For a few months, I did my best to disappear from the city.

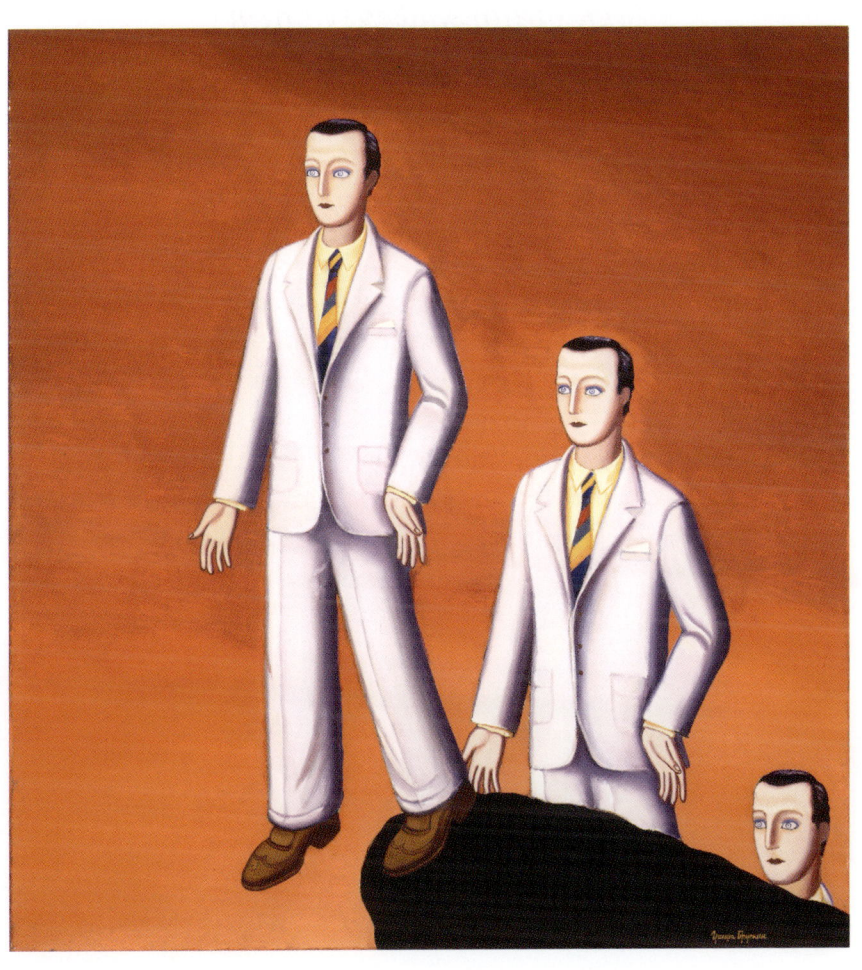

Grisha Bruskin, *Fragment*, oil on linen.

I'm Off to Madrid to Kick
the Ass of That Communist Bitch

In the West, Edik organized a battle for the liberation of his wife.

One day in my apartment the phone rang. I picked up the receiver and heard what seemed to be the voice of my friend, quite smashed.

"Grishutka," he said, "I'm going to Madrid to kick the ass of that Communist bitch Dolores Ibarrury. Tell the general that I will not stop defaming your country until he lets Tatyana go."

I kept silent as the grave.

The next day the telephone ceased showing any signs of life.

The Anti-Soviet Bastards

At that time, Alesya and I were living with her father.

An invalid on crutches, with only one leg, my father-in-law maintained contact with the outside world, including his publishers, exclusively by telephone.

Calling the local phone station from a neighbor's and not getting a clear answer, he decided he might as well blame the Soviet State, in which nothing ever worked.

My wife and I headed for the head of Moscow Telephone, to shake out the truth.

Entering his office, we asked the telephone boss what had happened to our equipment. We didn't forget to mention Alesya's invalid father, a veteran of the Great Patriotic War.

The boss found it hard to come to terms with the notion that the anti-Soviet bastards had fathers. He reported:

"Your telephone has been disconnected. For six months. In conjunction with the law that provides for the use of such measures in response to the holding of telephone conversations of anti-Soviet or antisocial character."

Say, for Example, You Shove Somebody on the Street

"Do you mean to say that you're listening illegally to people's telephone conversations?" we asked.

"Nothing of the kind," retorted the boss. "The character of a person's telephone conversation can be judged from his social behavior. Say, for example, you shove somebody on the street, or after leaving here you meet with a foreign journalist to tell him about the subject of our conversation. Keep in mind, this is just a preventative measure."

Precisely six months later a workman came to us from the telephone station and said:

"People have been complaining that they can't reach you."

He unscrewed the phone, tugged some wires for form's sake, and the telephone rang.

The Wife of an Enemy of the USSR

Growing desperate after several years of battles with the KGB and threats from them of the sort: "Tatyana Ivanovna, we'll let you go when you get old and aren't any use to anyone," Tanya decided on a hunger strike.

Death or freedom!

Having experience with prolonged fasting, I tried to give advice and provide appropriate literature.

On the twenty-fifth day Tanya's health deteriorated. A doctor was needed.

My friend, the dissident Volodya Tolts, advised getting Elena Bonner, a doctor by profession.

At the apartment, Elena Bonner was met by Tanya's worried mother, Margarita Ivanovna, who had come to see her sick daughter. The friendly, knowledgeable doctor struck her as very nice indeed.

The general's lady could not fathom that before her was the wife of Andrei Sakharov, Internal Enemy of the USSR Number One.

The General's Fighting Heart

On the thirty-third day, the general was told that because of an anti-Soviet propaganda coup, organized by enemy forces, he could lose his daughter.

The general's fighting heart gave a shudder.

He sent his own trusted doctor, by all appearances a Party member, who confirmed that his offspring was on the brink of death.

Sacrificing his promotion, the subjugator of Prague committed a humanitarian act and let Tanya and her baby go.

When times changed in Russia, the general organized a joint business with the Colt company. He even traveled to Prague to formally ask Duběk's forgiveness.

The BBC recorded the touching scene.

The general got his royalties.

"Them"

When I got to America, I went to Washington and stayed with Tanya and Edik.

At that time Tanya's mother was with them.

She asked whether I had gotten the money from the sale of my paintings at the Sotheby auction in Moscow. Hearing that I hadn't, the general's lady got indignant.

"What! *They* didn't pay you? You have to struggle with *them*. You have to sue *them* in court."

I was dumbstruck. For me, "they" meant nobody so much as generals in the USSR.

The Head's Behind the Frame

We needed to have bookshelves built.

We hired a carpenter, Aleksey Ivanovich.

Seeing an etching on the wall, a gift from Ernst Neizvestny, he asked:

"What's this? A painting?"

"You decide," said my wife.

"Right, a painting. Looks like a woman. And the head's behind the frame."

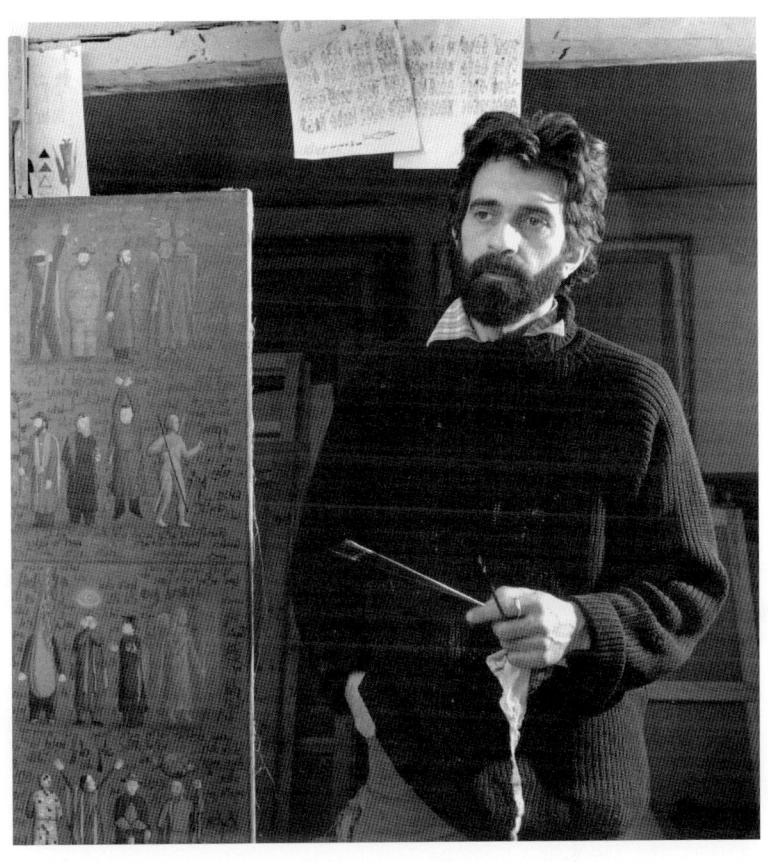

In the Mayakovsky Square studio, Moscow, 1983.
Photograph by Yury Zheltov.

Aleksey Ivanovich and a Pair of Glasses

One day Aleksey Ivanovich complained that he couldn't see.

"You need glasses," I advised.

"I have glasses. I bought them for nothing off my nephew. But they don't help," said the carpenter.

I Got Drunk and Dropped Like a Stick

Alesya asked:

"Why didn't you show up? We waited for you the whole day."

"I got drunk and dropped like a stick," reported the craftsman.

A Foreign Name

Aleksey Ivanovich considered:

"There's something I don't understand. You, Aleska, are Russian. Grigor Ivanych is Russian. Tyomka is Russian. But your mother has a foreign name, Safo."

My mother-in-law really had the foreign name Safo.

Give Me a Piece of Candy

Around New Year's, Aleksey Ivanovich finished his job and came to get paid.

When he saw chocolate candies among the ornaments on the New Year's tree, he said:

"Give me a piece of candy."

Alesya held out a bowl.

"No, give me one from the tree," he said.

So Very Contented

Igor worked with Alesya in the editorial office.

Igor was over six feet tall and swarthy. With his almond-shaped eyes and pitch-black hair and beard, a priest's cylindrical hat crowning his small head, he looked like a Persian prince and stood out like a bright spot in the northern Moscow crowd.

Editing atheistic texts, Igor, in defiance of Soviet rules, would neatly adjust every appearance of the word "God" so it started with a capital letter.

He promised Alesya instantaneous healing from all misfortunes if she became Russian Orthodox.

Sometimes he would sit next to her and say:

"Oh, what a blessing it is to look at you: You sit and you knit. And you're so slim, and your hair is so smooth. And I'm so peaceful. So very quiet. So very contented."

Not Without Success

When Igor's wife died he realized an old dream and took the vows of a monk.

Living in the monastery, he found a way to "satisfy the flesh" and secretly married.

The deception came to light. There was a scandal. Igor was kicked out of the monastery in disgrace.

Not batting an eyelid, he became a movie actor.

Apparently not without success.

We'll Be Perfectly Comfortable

In the fall of 1985, I went to an artists' retreat in Tarusa.

In Tarusa we were met by the new director, a retired colonel who had just been appointed to the post. In his accustomed style, he ordered the artists to stand in alphabetic order to have their names called.

There was friendly laughter.

A few days later my wife came from Moscow to visit me.

Seeing us out on a walk, the ex-commander jabbed a finger in Alesya's direction and barked:

"Who's this?"

I answered that this was my wife.

"Where are you going to sleep?" he asked.

"In the room assigned to me," I said.

"But you only have a single cot there. You'll be uncomfortable," persisted the guardian of military morals.

"We'll be perfectly comfortable," we answered in chorus.

Whose Agent Are You?
Who Are You Working For?

The other unpleasant character at the retreat was the group leader, the old artist Motorin.

All his life he painted the same insipid still life with a joint of meat and a shot glass.

From time to time Motorin would check in on the artists' studios, to exercise his leadership. I avoided him as best I could.

Finally he paid a visit to my studio.

Looking at my work, the old man turned around and, screwing up his eyes as though shooting a pistol, wheezed in a high-pitched old man's falsetto:

"Whose agent are you? Who are you working for?"

"The agent of Art. Working for Eternity," I retorted without thinking.

It's So Noble

The mother of a friend of mine, a woman with a good income, found out that I didn't have the money to buy canvas and exclaimed:

"Poverty, Grisha, it's so noble."

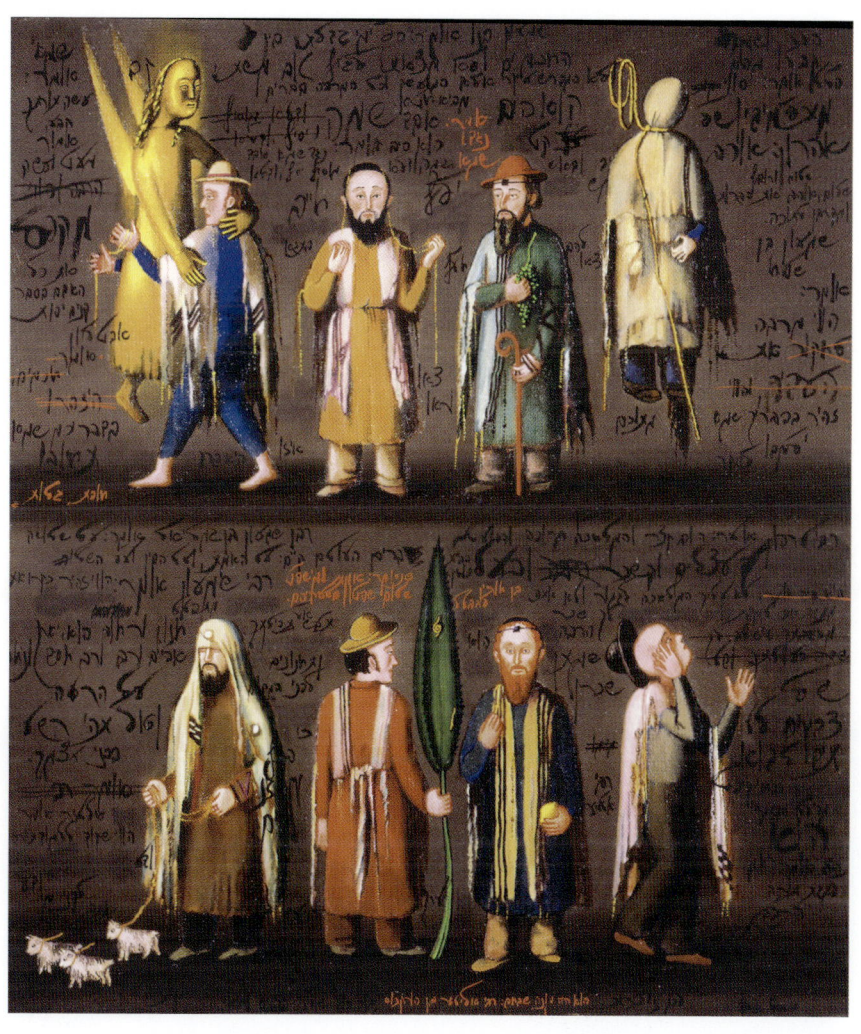

Grisha Bruskin, *Alefbet 4*, oil on linen.

Like a Dirty Sock

My Hebrew teacher, Senya, got baptized.

After some time he recognized that he had made a false step. He decided to return to Judaism and get circumcised.

He made arrangements with a surgeon friend of his.

The operation was done in secret. In the teacher's kitchen.

To get his courage up, the patient was given a stiff drink. After which he was hoisted onto the kitchen table, cleared for the occasion. Senya's wife, Asya, bravely assisted, handing over the scalpel, tweezers, cotton, iodine, and so forth.

Following the operation, Senya was in serious pain.

After a few days of torment, he called the doctor.

"Listen, buddy, it's swollen, the stitches look awful, it keeps hurting. I could die! What should I do?"

"Wash it like a dirty sock and put it to use," advised the doctor.

A Worthy Response

Some friends of ours asked their son Grisha, a fourth grader, to show them his report card.

"Tactless bastards," objected the knowledgeable young scholar.

A Businessman

We rented a dacha in Vnukovo.

Our landlord was a tall, handsome, but rather thickheaded non-entity, who went around with strange ideas.

One day he said to me:

"Grisha, you can't make a living with your brush. Let's raise pigs!" (He said *chazers*, from Yiddish.) "At the end of the summer, you'll have yourself a car, and I'll have myself a car."

In the meantime, the landlord had put his hopes in zucchini, which he had planted on both sides of the narrow path leading from the gate to the house.

Watering his income every day, the "businessman" dreamed that there would be a huge harvest, and that at the end of the summer he would be rich.

Wonderful News

The artist Natasha Nesterova rented a dacha not too far away. The owners were Zosya and Boris.

All their animals had the patronymic Borisovich. For example, the cat was Vasil Borisovich and the piglet was Boris Borisovich.

One evening Natasha and Zosya came over.

Zosya was bringing us a bowl of meat jelly. Still at the door she declared:

"We have wonderful news! Lyovochka (Natasha's son) got into college!" And then, pointing at the meat jelly, "Boris Borisovich has met his end! Try Boris Borisovich!"

We celebrated the happy event with vodka and Boris Borisovich.

Late at night, teetering unsteadily, the guests went home.

Early in the morning I stuck my nose out the door and saw a "landscape after the battle," littered with slaughtered zucchini.

An Unknown Person

I got a call from an unknown person who told me in French that he had brought a couple of videocassettes as a present from a childhood friend who was now living in Washington.

We agreed to meet at the entrance to the Mayakovsky metro station, which was in the same building as my studio.

At some point an out-of-breath man appeared, looking apprehensively from one side to another.

"I've got a tail," he said. "The whole way from the hotel I've been followed by a stranger with a blue plastic bag."

Looking around and not seeing anything suspicious, I decided that the young man, frightened by stories about the ubiquitous Soviet secret services, just saw KGB agents everywhere.

We went to the studio.

When I learned that my guest was the chairman of the youth division of the Christian Democratic Party, I understood that his fears were not unjustified.

The chairman handed me a present and asked if I didn't have a priest among my friends.

I answered in the affirmative and received in return a heavy box of religious books and a packet of brochures, after which the young man took his leave.

The Very Image of the Thief

It was summer, and my wife and I were getting ready to go from the studio right to the dacha.

I had taken from home a pair of not-so-innocent books for our son, Tyoma: Solzhenitsyn and Avtorkhanov. Packing the books into a bag of gifts, we set off for the metro.

At the ticket booth two policeman walked up to us and asked for our documents.

To the question "why," the guardians of Soviet order informed us that a lady had just reported that her bag was stolen. That bag looked just like our bag, and I matched her description: the very image of the thief.

Calculating in my head how many years we were going to pay for trying to educate our son, I lost myself in speculation regarding those mysterious leaflets.

Paralyzed with fear I held out my passport. The cop neatly wrote the data into his little book.

"And now your documents," he turned menacingly to my wife, who, it appeared, also had a thievish look.

Having obtained the information they desired, to our great relief the cops took off.

The Blue Bag

In the metro car I was struck by an unprepossessing man holding a blue plastic bag.

We decided to get off at the next stop. "Blue Bag" got off after us.

On our trail, "Bag" followed us into the next train.

Remembering detective novels we had read, we made a series of clever maneuvers, lifted from that suddenly useful literature, and finally shook him.

When we arrived at the dacha we decided to listen to the news.

The announcer was reading off the main event of the day: a demonstration of fascist thugs from the despicable Christian Democratic Party in support of the antipatriotic Polish Solidarity movement had ended in a dirty scuffle with the justifiably indignant simple Soviet people who were helping out at the Goodwill Games at Moscow's Olympic Stadium.

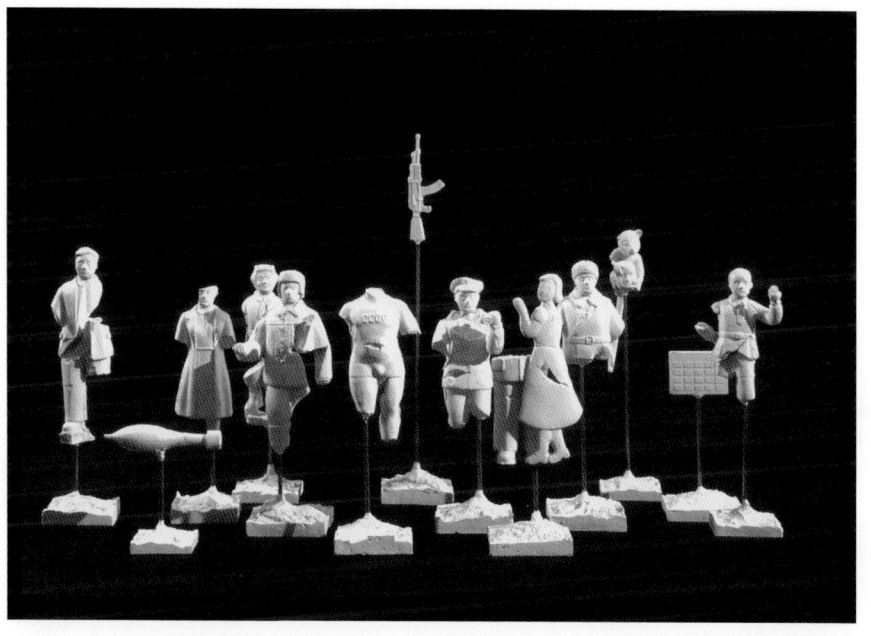

Grisha Bruskin, *An Archeologist's Collection* (fragment), painted bronze.

They Checked under the Bed

One day I got a call from the office of a newly arrived *New York Times* correspondent, the latest in a series accredited to Moscow.

The journalist said that he had brought me a letter and wanted to give it to me.

We met at the Mayakovsky monument and set off for my studio. We talked about one thing and the other, and parted.

After the American left, my students arrived. I was coaching them on the correct way to paint and draw for the entrance exam to the Art Institute.

Suddenly the door to our peaceful art school shook with a deafening knock.

Opening it, I stood face-to-face with the police. I figured that the new correspondent's KGB tail had sent an exploratory party to check out whom the *Times* was visiting.

Pushing me inside and telling an astonishingly suspenseful story—apparently, an apartment in the next building had been robbed, and the robber, chased by the police, had taken cover in an entryway, or even in my studio, the cops demanded to see my documents in order to establish my clearly suspicious identity.

When they entered the room and discovered the dumbstruck adolescents, the law-enforcement agents made a show of inspecting the corners.

Nor did they forget to check under the bed.

The Sleuth

At the beginning of the 1980s, my good friend, the art historian Bob Brodsky, brought to my studio a Swiss television producer, Erik Peshler.

Erik became my collector and my friend.

As he was filming a documentary about Soviet life, he often came to Moscow, and every time he would carry off a small painting in his suitcase.

On this ill-fated evening, since he was in town, Peshler came to get a painting from me.

Packing it safely, I looked into the courtyard and exchanged glances with a strange individual who was pacing underneath my windows.

A half hour later, Erik and I gave another look down below. The individual was still at his post.

We had to wait.

A Far-Gone Alcoholic

Our plans had been to go from the studio to a friend of Erik's, the composer Kataev, who lived nearby.

My wife, Alesya, was planning on joining us. She had directions, in which a liquor store figured prominently.

After calling the Kataevs a few times and hearing that we hadn't arrived, she began to worry. Finally, unable to stand it, she set off for the studio, which didn't have a telephone.

At exactly this moment under cover of night the tail made himself invisible.

We took the rolled-up canvas and, looking carefully around us, finally set off for our destination, just missing my wife.

At two in the morning, finding nobody in the studio, Alesya, breathing hard, with her sheepskin coat undone, tore off in search of the Kataevs' building.

When, accidentally, she ran into a friend of ours, she forgot even to say hello.

"Where's the liquor store here?" she shrieked in panic, leaving him with the impression of a far-gone alcoholic.

The Accent of a German Prisoner of War

A few days later, Peshler flew off to Switzerland.

As a VIP, he never had to show his bags at customs.

This time, however, the customs officer asked to see the contents of his suitcase. Finding the painting, he demanded an explanation, threatening to bring in expert appraisers.

In broken Russian, with the accent of a German prisoner of war, Erik noisily insisted that he had bought the painting in the Izmailovo flea market for three rubles and was bringing it home to show his children the happy lives of young pioneers in the USSR.

The abundance of explanations and gesticulations overwhelmed the mistrustful agent, who finally gave up in disgust and said:

"Go through."

The Ghost

A few years later, in New York, I visited the Soviet Mission to the UN on Sixty-seventh Street.

The Russian consulate was then located in Washington, and the only place to notarize the Soviet document I needed was this rather gloomy establishment.

My business over, I set off for home, lost in thought.

On the way, seemingly from underground, there materialized a ghost: a man in sports clothes holding a tennis racket.

With a big smile, the putative athlete asked me how to get to Grand Central Station, from where, it seemed, he was traveling to a tennis match.

I explained.

"Where did you get that delightful accent?" inquired the stranger.

I answered.

Not satisfied, and with an insistence uncharacteristic of Americans in such situations, the tennis player continued to interrogate me.

"Nice weather, isn't it? Where are you going?"

Understanding, at long last, whom I was dealing with, I told him to go to hell.

The ghost magically vanished.

In a Free Country

Continuing my journey, I decided to go home by cab and started hailing one.

Three policemen walked up and asked to see my papers. Since I was in a free country, I freely asked what right they had.

To my astonishment, I heard a painfully familiar story. A store across the street had been robbed, and the thief could have been my twin, his jacket was just like my jacket, you couldn't tell them apart.

Apparently, the Soviet Mission to the UN was under surveillance, and the FBI, gathering information about visitors to this "bad" house, used methods identical to those of the KGB.

Come Closer, I'll Make You Three Feet Tall

At seventeen, Lyokha went to prison. While he hadn't himself participated in the robbery, he had organized it.

When he came out, Alesya's parents did their best to help him.

Lyokha sang terrific criminal songs, accompanying himself on the guitar. He became a student at the Literary Institute.

Unconventional Lyokha made a strong impression on anyone he came in contact with.

Grateful to Alesya's parents, he'd tell them,

"You took me in naked. If someone insults you, I'll come and kick the door in with my ass."

If he didn't like somebody:

"You're six feet tall? Come closer, I'll make you three feet tall."

Intimate relations he described succinctly as "pulling out the mattress."

Once, arriving with his lady, he said:

"Elena Nikolaevna and I are in a hurry to fulfill our plans. While Pop's out, do you think we could crash in his study?" She had, he explained respectfully, a master's degree.

Asked to Go to Make Pee-Pee

I had a student named Sveta.

One day Sveta appeared with a tear-stained face and told me in despair that her husband, involved in an illegal business, had gotten into a mess. His family was in danger. Going to the police was out of the question.

We remembered Lyokha.

He came that very evening.

To Alesya's question of where he'd been all this time, he informed us:

"The cops came. I asked to go to make pee-pee and swallowed my address book. What if they decided to look you up: you've got Nabokov here, and Solzhenitsyn, and you just lie around, playing guitar and smoking joints?"

Dinosaur

Once on a visit from New York to Moscow I telephoned Lyokha.

We met.

When we parted, he handed me a set of painted Russian souvenirs and said:

"Grisha, dinosaurs are extinct, but I'm still here. If you need something, call."

He Snitched

In 1983, the Latvian Artists Union invited me to hold an exhibition in Vilnius.

The Union's liberal chairman, a man named Talberg, had given his approval.

The opening took place toward the end of July.

Opinions in the guest book were contradictory, ranging from exultation ("My thanks to the artist, Now I can go through life with my head held high." Shapiro) to open threats ("Mr. Bruskin, take down your paintings and go home before you get arrested." A Lithuanian Woman).

A week later, the head of the Division of Ideology of the Central Committee of the Communist Party of Lithuania, Comrade Shepetis, paid a visit to the exhibition. Not liking what he found, he gave orders to close it. At the same time, he snitched to the Moscow Committee.

The Moscow Artists Union was reproached for its ideological lapse and advised to "take measures."

The leadership of the Artists Union called me in to a jury of peers and demanded, on the counsel of the Lithuanian ideologue, that I present the evidence: the painting *In Red Space* and the guest book.

Editing the guest book by cutting out the pages with threats and adding some "good" responses, I appeared at the kangaroo court.

A performance began that was worthy of Ionesco.

Humanity in Danger

The Management was not sure what to indict me with, "Zionism" or "Anti-Soviet activity."

They decided on both.

All the judges were artists who worked in administration. They demanded an explanation of the meaning of the painting and its red background.

In response I mumbled some generalities about humanity.

One of the party bosses then observed that all of this was rooted in the ideology of existentialism, proclaimed by the politically illiterate French philosopher Jean-Paul Sartre and alien to the Soviet people.

Another administrator drew his colleagues' attention to that fact that the red background on the painting was nothing other than a travesty of the sacred red banner, and that the people depicted in the painting betray the artist's malicious intent: to ridicule the noble Soviet people, the builders of Communism.

Finally, a third bureaucrat asked in a menacing tone if I had read yesterday's newspapers. On hearing a negative response, he exploded:

"You should have. The world, for your information, is on the brink of atomic war. The Americans are rattling their weapons. Humanity is in danger. While you permit yourself *this!*"

At the word *this* I was told to step outside. The trial was over.

The sentence: a public reprimand.

Look, Old Man, I Hope You Understood

Oddly enough, the man who reminded us of the American threat ran into me a little later in lobby of the building. Making sure that nobody was around, he said:

"Look, old man, I hope you understood that I did everything I could to save you. You were your own worst enemy: instead of lying low and keeping quiet, you kept on objecting. Everybody saw that you didn't acknowledge your own guilt."

In fact, the person who did the saving was the artist Igor Popov, who headed the Moscow Artists Union after the death of Talberg. When he was pressured from above and below to kick me out of the Union, he responded that he would strip himself of the authority to act in the case.

Popov was acting, as the phrase goes, according to his conscience. At the same time, he obviously didn't want to create a dangerous precedent for the organization he headed.

I am still grateful to this honorable man.

Blacklisted

In 1984, I was supposed to have an exhibition in the Central Artists House. The planning had gone on for several years.

The House leadership knew nothing about my Lithuanian battles.

Friends in the know from the Exhibition Committee advised me to choose my works with care, which I did.

The exhibition opened with appropriate fanfare to a large crowd. As was the custom at the time, there was a heated discussion of the paintings on exhibit, followed by a banquet in a local restaurant.

When I came to the Artists House the next day, I found the doors to the exhibition hall locked.

It turned out that at nine o'clock in the morning that same day, the Party's City Council had held a meeting in the same building. On the agenda was the intensification of ideological work in the cultural field.

The Council's chairman for ideology, Comrade Rogozhin, gave a report that used Bruskin's insolent exhibition in Vilnius as an example of serious ideological error. He described the artist's works in a way that, from a Party standpoint, was highly uncomplimentary.

At eleven A.M., the front doors were opened wide.

At twelve, committee members with Rogozhin at their head went out for lunch and saw, before their very noses, the criminal exhibition of the ideological enemy.

There was a scandal. The exhibition was closed immediately. The management of Artists House was removed.

I was permanently blacklisted.

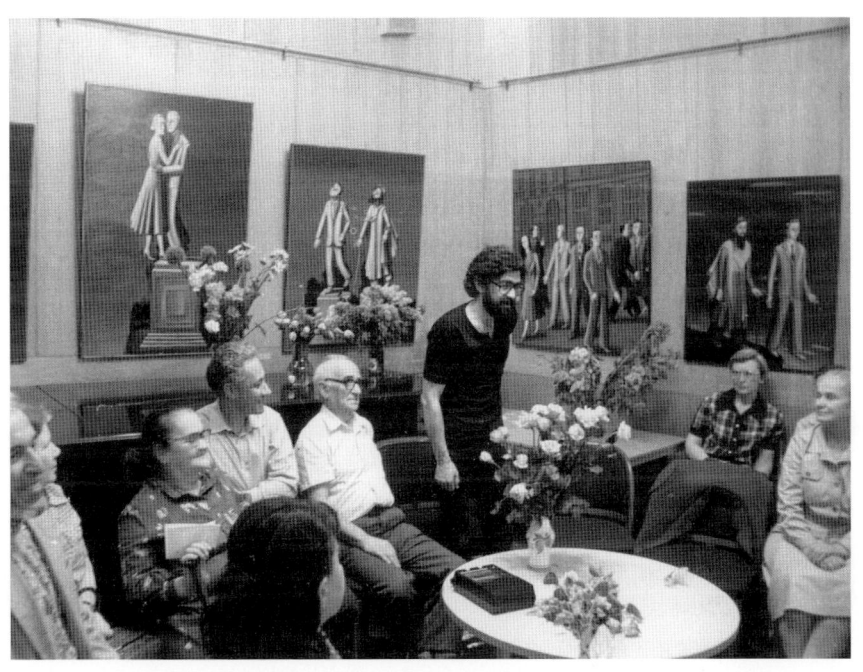

The opening of the exhibition in the Central Artists House, Moscow, 1984.
Photograph by V. Kravchuk.

The Faithful Leninist

In 1985, the faithful Leninist Gorbachev came to power in Russia.

After ordering the Soviet people to give up their vodka for yogurt and act responsibly, he declared glasnost and perestroika.

Nobody took the newcomer seriously: it was common for Soviet leaders to proclaim a new stage in the development of socialism on its inexorable victorious march to communism.

It looked like the usual rejuvenating makeup on the face of the same old geezer.

Up to 1987, Russia was as always cut off from the world by the notorious Iron Curtain.

Culture remained under strict ideological control.

The country held pompous thematic exhibitions, timed to coincide with glorious Bolshevik holidays.

An Uninformed Public

Prigov called and said that Moscow Television wanted to do a feature on new lesser-known poets: Prigov, Rubinshtein, Gandlevsky, and Kibirov.

Sanych, as I called Prigov, proposed that they do the filming in my studio on Mayakovsky Square. He had the devious idea of using my paintings as background, in that way informing the public about my existence.

I set up the "background" in the form of *Fundamental Lexicon* and at the appointed time welcomed a team of cameramen accompanied by the servants of the Muse.

Not knowing whose studio it was, the lady director turned to the head cameraman and said in a loud voice in my presence:

"Make sure these lousy paintings don't show up in the picture."

The public remained uninformed.

Regenerated Precepts

In February 1987, a group of artists decided to organize a public show at the Kashirka Street Exhibition Hall called "The Artist and Modernity."

Invitations to participate were extended to those who for one reason or another had not followed the precepts of socialist realism and so had been unable to show their work.

At that time Gorbachev was demonstrating to the world his good will and regenerated Communist precepts by holding a pompous conference in Moscow, the so-called "Forum for a Non-Nuclear World."

He invited all sorts of well-known activists in politics, religion, and the arts.

Among those who came were Friedrich Durenmatt, Max Frisch, Yoko Ono, and Miloš Forman.

Using the services of translators we knew, we tried to let the attendees know that an alternative art exhibition was being held. We personally invited the aforementioned celebrities to the opening.

We agreed among ourselves that if the authorities wanted to remove any work whatsoever, then all the artists would take their paintings off the walls.

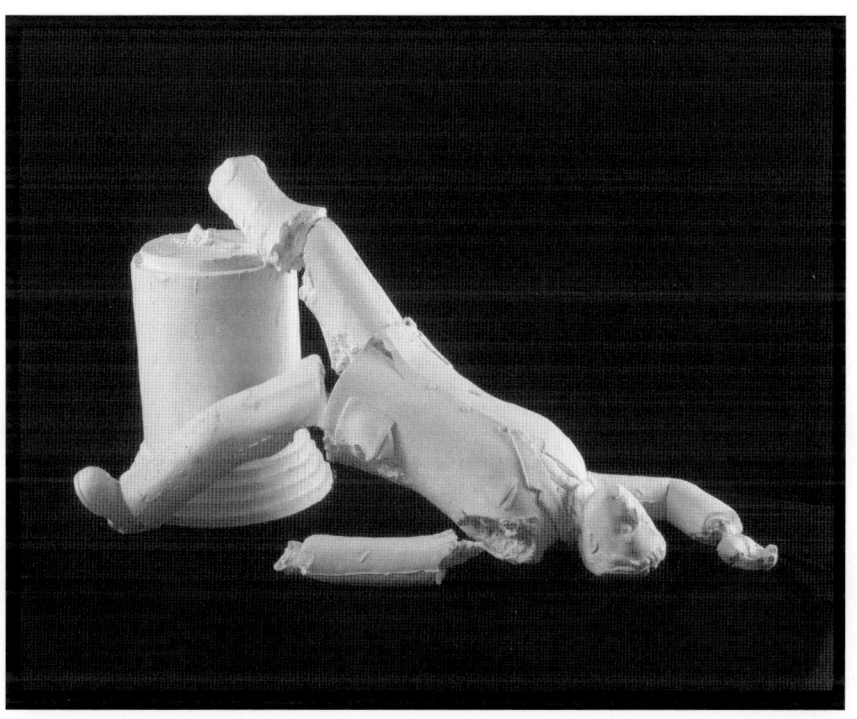

Grisha Bruskin, *The Fall*, painted bronze.

The Priestesses of Authority

As was customary, when the exhibition was ready, censorship arrived in the form of two ideological ladies from the Ministry of Culture. Their task was to assert Party control.

The priestesses of authority demanded that we exclude two works from the collection on exhibit. Their Party morality was offended by Yankilevsky's *Light and Darkness*, in the center of which was a mutant with a head growing out of his anus.

Their political sensibilities were scandalized by my *Fundamental Lexicon*.

A Valuable Directive

Informing the ladies that the entire cultural beau monde from the ongoing Gorbachev conference had been invited, the artist-organizers refused to remove the works.

We stood our ground, threatening an international scandal: the world would learn what Gorbachev's glasnost really meant, just more cheating and stage decorations.

I have to say that at that moment the cultural bureaucrats were truly flustered: they lacked "valuable directives" from above. Nobody knew where the wind would blow from the next second.

In the end, a valuable directive was issued from the ministerial Olympus by the then Minister of Culture.

Moscow saw the opening of its first independent uncensored exhibition.

First of All, There's No Composition to Speak Of

The day after the opening, the artist Nina Sergeeva, a member of the Party's Section on Painting, strolled through the exhibition halls. She was wearing a white canvas cap; a painter's case was slung across her shoulder.

Seeing me, she snapped:

"So where are your works?"

I pointed to *Fundamental Lexicon.*

"Very bad!" said Nina. "First of all, there's no composition to speak of. Second of all, the white doesn't go with the background. Third of all, you live here and don't know anything, and I've traveled the whole world. In artistic terms, this is yesterday. The West experienced this a long time ago."

Proletarian Opinions

The exhibition became a sensation in Moscow. In front of the hall stood long lines of culture-starved Muscovites along with curiosity seekers and comrades eager to look and condemn.

The local party bosses decided to protect themselves in case the government rolled back glasnost.

Buses started appearing in front of the exhibition hall, packed with cadres from local factories.

The masses expressed their honest proletarian opinions on the pages of the guest book.

Here and there somebody issued a threat. I cite verbatim the comments of a sweet proletarian girl: "As for the artist Kabakov, I would shoot him with my own hands with a machine gun, and I'd smear him over his own white canvas."

A Strange Organization

In 1987, I saw a videocassette of the film *One Flew Over the Cuckoo's Nest*, forbidden in the USSR. It made a big impression on me.

When on the eve of the exhibition I read in the paper that Miloš Forman was coming to Russia for the Gorbachev conference, I told my wife that this was a man to whom I'd like to show the *Fundamental Lexicon*.

Forman came to the exhibition, and we met.

The director turned out to be an exceptionally kind and vibrant person. It was easy and interesting to talk to him.

Miloš expressed an interest in acquiring two paintings from the exhibition: my *Fundamental Lexicon* and a work of Andrei Grositsky entitled *The Window*.

For that purpose, on the following day we all set off for an organization with the strange name "InterBook." Among other activities—probably arms dealing—it managed the foreign export of works of art.

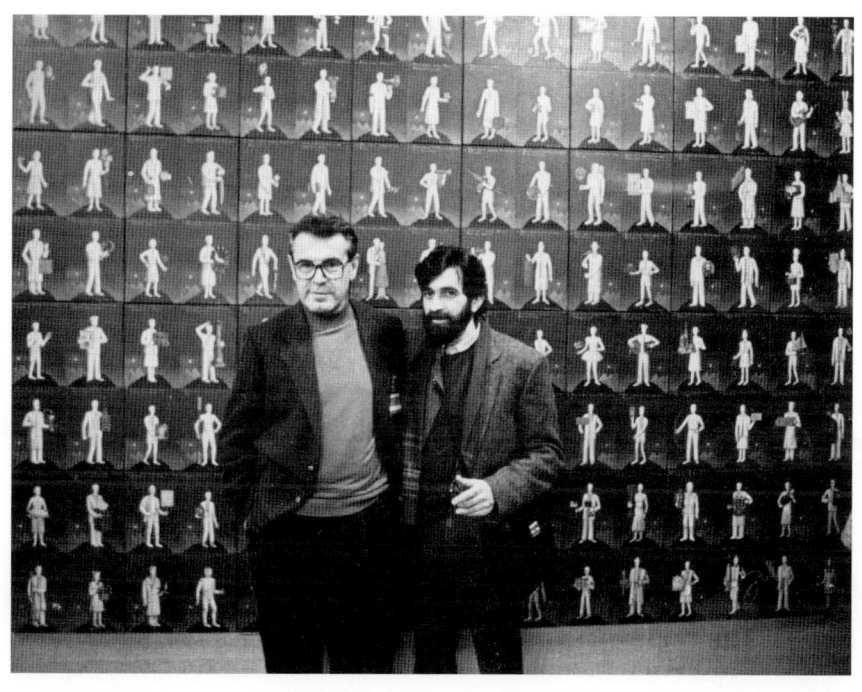

With Miloš Forman, Moscow, 1987.

Mister Twister

InterBook was guarded on the scale of a medieval castle.

At the entrance our path was blocked by police.

I have to say that their gaze fell upon a suspicious-looking crew. Andrei and I, two scandalous, bohemian, "unorthodox" artists, hardly aroused their trust. The translator was an ordinary Soviet woman. Finally there was Miloš Forman, a Hollywood star who not so long ago had been persona non grata in the USSR.

Dressed from head to foot in leather and fox fur, with an expensive cigar in his mouth, Forman stood out in dreary winter-gray Moscow like the capitalist from the children's classic *Mister Twister*.

From the entryway we telephoned the man we needed. We told him who we were and explained our business.

Apparently, our appearance caused a departmental commotion.

The comrades spent a long time conferring with one another and with the corresponding "organs." Kick us out or let us in? Permit it or forbid it?

Finding It Without Artistic Value

Finally, after a wait of an hour and a half, we were politely invited to proceed to the appropriate room.

The bureaucrats, following their new instructions and refraining from complicating international relations, approved the purchase.

The price was supposed to be set by the Arts Council of the Ministry of Culture. The Council appraised my painting at two thousand rubles (three hundred dollars), finding it without particular artistic value.

The second half of that painting, a work of the same dimensions, was sold a year and a half later at the first (and last) Sotheby Moscow Auction for $416,000.

All I Did Was Piss

One day there was a knock on my studio door.

Opening it up, I discovered a young man with a classic Scottish look.

The visitor was the Moscow correspondent of the British paper *The Guardian*. Saying that he wanted to interview me, he walked into the studio.

By way of establishing friendly relations, the correspondent reached in his pocket for a flask of cognac. He said that we were of the same generation and undoubtedly shared many interests. For example, cricket.

After the cognac, he asked to use the toilet. When he came out, I showed him where he could wash his hands.

"Thanks, that won't be necessary," said the Scotsman. "All I did was piss."

The Symbols and the Key

A certain western curator came to get my advice on participants in an exhibition he was thinking of organizing. He showed me a list.

I said that since I was an artist myself, I couldn't provide an opinion.

When, out of curiosity, I glanced at the list, I noticed that opposite every name was a symbol: a check mark, a plus, a minus, a little circle.

At the bottom of the list was an explanation:

Check mark: genius

Plus: talented

Minus: mediocre

Little circle: hopeless

Noticing the astonishment on my face, the guest explained that he had met a lady "close to artistic circles" who, wishing to be helpful, had provided the symbols and the key.

A Bit on the Expensive Side

After the exhibition on Kashirka Street a nice Greek journalist by the name of Guerassimus appeared in my studio.

He wanted to buy a small painting. I named the price: four hundred dollars.

Handing over the money, the journalist threw me a piteous look and said that it was a bit on the expensive side. I gave him back half.

That evening my wife and I went to Kutuzovsky Prospect, and I gave him the painting.

The weather was awful, we were freezing, and decided to take a cab or hail a private car. Nobody stopped.

Finally, at the end of her rope, Alesya got out the money and shouted:

"Malaya Gruzinskaya, two hundred dollars!"

An Effusive Italian

I never valued or paid attention to the sketches that I made for my works in great quantity.

Then I was introduced to an effusive man, a political advisor to the Italian ambassador in Russia.

Visiting me in the studio and learning that I wasn't selling any paintings, he turned his attention to a sketch tacked to the wall. I gave it to him.

Three days later, the Italian came again.

"Old man, I'm crazy about that gift, I gave it the place of honor in my flat. Do you have anything else?"

I got out a huge file.

"How much?" asked the advisor, choosing a few sheets.

I named a symbolic price.

A few days later the guest was back.

"Old man, your sketches have brought beauty to my life. I want to buy another dozen."

"What do you want to do, sell them?"

"God forbid! I have a large collection of graphics in Rome. The sketches will become a worthy part of it."

The Italian chose a dozen sketches.

Exactly one week later my admirer appeared again.

"Grisha, you can't imagine what's happening to me. I can't tear myself away from your sketches. I want to buy more."

When I understood that I was dealing with a crook, I absolutely refused.

He saw a new sketch on the table and started in again.

In order to get rid of him, I named a price that for that time was outrageous: a thousand dollars. Without a murmur, the Italian held out the required sum.

After that, I started treating my drawings with greater care.

Bruskin: Guggenheim

Through InterBook I met a Western businessman who was actively buying the work of unofficial artists.

When he saw the second half of *Fundamental Lexicon*, he said:

"Grisha, you shouldn't give this work to the Sotheby auction. Sell it to me, and it will hang in the best museum in the world, the Guggenheim."

I asked for proof. The businessman took out a file folder, opened it, and held it out to me.

I saw a computer print-out:

Kalinin: Tate Gallery

Plavinsky: Washington National Gallery

Steinberg: Museum of Modern Art

Yankilevsky: Metropolitan

Bulatov: Frick

Purygin: Centre Pompidou

Finally I got to myself—Bruskin: Guggenheim.

I kicked him out.

Everything's under Control

On June 1, 1988, in the same Kashirka Street exhibition hall mentioned earlier, I staged *The Birth of a Hero* as performance art.

In accordance with the script, I had on my arm the red band of the People's Militia patrol.

Right before the performance, I went out for a smoke.

A police car drove up, summoned by some well-wisher. Taking me for a real vigilante, the cop asked:

"So what's going on there?"

"Everything's under control," I answered honestly.

The cops sped off.

Fascists

The exhibition "The Artist and Modernity" stirred the sleeping ant-heap of Moscow artistic life.

At the exhibition, for the first time in my life I met an art dealer, the genial Chicago gallery owner Bill Struve. We began to work together.

Sensing the fresh air, Western collectors, art dealers, and curators descended on Moscow.

For their part, government officials figured out that this disreputable art could bring in some good money.

The Berne Museum of Art decided to organize an exhibition of the Moscow Underground. In conjunction with this, the museum director, Hans-Christof von Tauvel, flew to Moscow.

Making the rounds of artist studios along with the Swiss diplomat Martin von Walterskirchen, he selected canvases, including my big painting *Logies*.

The exhibition would be called "I Live, I See," after a painting by Erik Bulatov.

The Ministry of Culture seized the opportunity and foisted on the Western guests a group of official artists.

The Swiss responded with a polite but firm refusal, after which the Ministry functionaries, searching for an appropriate epithet, started referring to them as fascists.

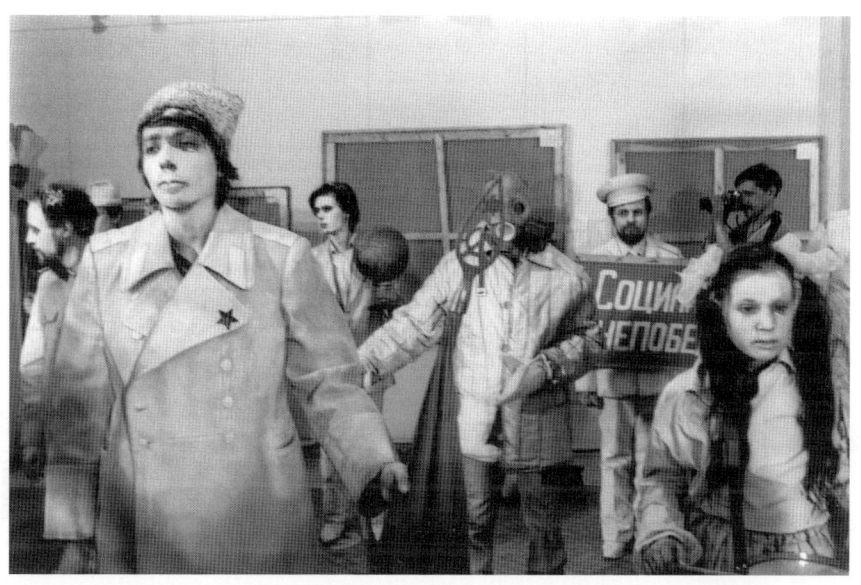

Performance of Grisha Bruskin, *Birth of a Hero*, Moscow, 1988.
Photograph by Sergey Borisov.

Glasnost Does Not Mean All Is Permitted

The selected works had to be approved by a Special Commission of the Ministry of Culture.

Not long before their meeting, I was summoned by a high-placed Ministry official, responsible for cultural export.

The official informed me that in yesterday's *Pravda*, Soviet people were put on notice that "glasnost does not mean all is permitted." He urged me to withdraw from the exhibition.

The country would not permit the export of ideas like that to the West.

A Devious Move

This would be my first museum exhibition, and I felt that it was very important to participate.

Von Tauvel and I conferred and decided on a devious move.

I made a soap solution and spread it on the thirty-five panels that composed the painting. Then I covered the detoxified surface with innocent themes in gouache.

A museum restorer arrived from Switzerland to photograph the fragments before and after.

The transformed work was presented to the Members of the High Commission, and deemed appropriate.

When the painting reached Berne, the restorer took warm water and cotton, removed the gouache, and easily restored the original.

True Spirituality

Edik Steinberg and his wife, Galya Manevich, were the first unofficial artists to go to Paris. The occasion was Edik's one-man exhibition at the Claude Bernard gallery.

On his return, he criticized France for the commercialization of art. But occasionally he would forget himself and adopt an ecstatic tone.

This reached such a pitch that, he'd suggest, it wouldn't be bad to go and live there for a while.

"Edik," Galya would remind him sternly, "true spirituality exists only in Russia."

He Made a Proposal

Steinberg was included in the exhibition "I Live, I See."

Deciding that his works were not going to be shown properly, he declined to participate.

Two *vons*, Messieurs von Tauvel and von Walterskirchen, paid him a visit at home to persuade him to change his mind.

Not knowing foreign languages, Edik asked Alesya to translate.

The visitors said that Steinberg was a wonderful and important artist, and that an exhibition without his works would be incomplete.

Alesya translated.

Having fortified himself a bit before the event, Edik turned to Alesya.

"Translate fuck off!"

Alesya translated:

"Mr. Steinberg thanks you very much, but considers his participation in the exhibition impossible."

À la Marina Abramovic

My studio was in the very center of Moscow, on Mayakovsky Square, in the attic of a three-story building dating from the time of Pushkin.

The entrance was from the courtyard, through the back staircase, and formed a stark contrast with the building's façade, which faced Gorky Street and was exceptionally attractive.

The courtyard's unimaginable filth, including a classic Gogolian puddle, was topped off with containers of gnawed-off bones à la Marina Abramovic, which had been carried there from the sausage store located on the ground floor.

Nasty gray rats periodically darted out of the containers into the yard and back again.

An Entrepreneur

The building was for the most part emptied out. For around thirty years it had been scheduled for demolition.

In my section of the building, in addition to myself, there lived in a deserted communal apartment a single tenant: Adelina Anisimovna Rubinshtein.

The old lady picked up promising-looking stray dogs from the street, with the idea of breeding pedigreed puppies, selling them, and making money.

The beginning was unusually successful. The dogs set to it and produced a dozen enchanting offspring.

Because of ill health, Adelina Anisimovna was not able to walk them. Instead of this, the aged entrepreneur would open the door and let them out.

Not being fools, the dogs decided to forgo a hopeless battle with the nasty rats and instead made use of our common staircase.

At first Rubinshtein tried to clean up after them. But she swiftly understood that it was beyond her abilities and threw up her hands.

A Minefield

At the start of the summer of 1988, I got a call from the Ministry of Culture. They arranged for me to host the distinguished collector Henry Nannen, former editor of the magazine *Der Stern*.

The visit was scheduled for 8:30 A.M.

At 8:25 I walked into the dark entryway and smelled something unpleasant. Further up, the staircase turned into a minefield. The dogs had apparently just walked themselves.

As it was too late to do anything, I entered the studio and started looking out the window for my guests.

A Foreign Footprint

Soon enough, a shining black government limousine sailed into the courtyard, dispersing the rats.

Out of the limousine emerged an elegantly dressed gentleman, accompanied by his secretary and a Ministry staff member.

To my relief, when the guests entered, I saw from their footprints that they had successfully negotiated the mine field.

The meeting went well. Touched by my works, his eyes full of tears, Nannen democratically but carelessly sat on the floor, the cleanliness of which left much to be desired.

He bought two paintings and took his leave.

Ten minutes later, armed with a flashlight, I examined the staircase.

In every dog pile I discovered the clear imprint of a foreign shoe.

Ger-Tsedek

I met a man with the aristocratic name Marek Pototsky.

Marek told me the history of his ancestor, who had lived in the seventeenth century.

The father of this man had sent him to Italy to study science and art. In the course of his travels he made the acquaintance of a religious Jew.

Talking with the Talmudist, the young Count Pototsky came to believe in the truth of the Hebrew Bible. He became a Jew.

Returning to his homeland many years later with the new name Abraham ben Abraham Ger-Tsedek, the former count became a *gabbai* at the Vilna synagogue.

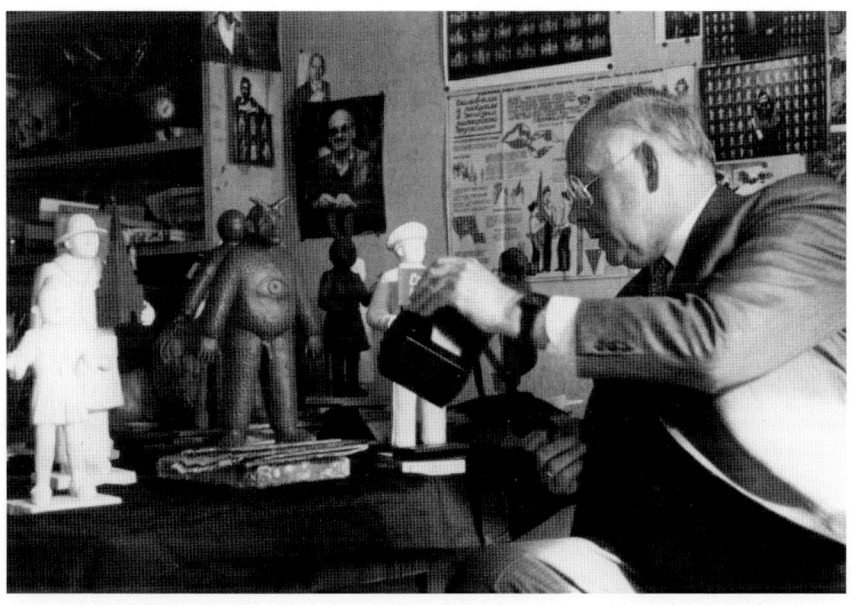

Collector Peter Ludwig at the Mayakovsky Square studio, 1988.

With a Prayer on His Lips

One day, Abraham ben Abraham upbraided a boy for inappropriate behavior in the synagogue.

The kid complained to his father. The father told the police.

Pototsky was arrested. He was thrown into a cell and then, in accordance with the custom of the age, taken to be burned alive.

Before his execution, the count was offered his life and his former high status in return for denouncing the Torah and the God of Abraham.

As the legend has it, the count stayed true to his chosen path and accepted a martyr's death.

With the prayer "Shma Yisroel" on his lips.

Market asked me to paint a picture for his collection, using the story of Ger-Tsedek.

His Ancestors Drank the Blood of Your Fathers

Marek grew up in Communist Poland.

One day his teacher walked into the classroom and commanded:

"Pototsky, stand up!" Pointing a finger at the boy, the pedagogue ran his eyes over the class and pronounced:

"Children, look at this boy. His ancestors drank the blood of your fathers and grandfathers."

As soon as it was possible, Marek escaped Poland for France.

I left for the West. We met. Marek said:

"Grisha, the greatest day of my life was not when I married Charlotte, and not when my children were born, but when I got a French passport."

The Gloom of the Studio

A businessman from Paris by the name of Alvarez appeared in Moscow.

He started buying up paintings by unofficial artists, explaining that he intended to donate his collection either to the Centre Pompidou or the Guggenheim. The artists got excited.

Meeting Alvarez at Edik Steinberg's exhibition, I arranged with him that following the banquet he'd come to my studio to look over my work.

Alvarez appeared at the banquet in the company of a lady with the impressive surname Rimsky-Korsakoff.

Late that night, my wife , Alvarez, and I set off for the studio along with Rimsky-Korsakoff.

Stepping into the entryway, we discovered that Soviet Power, playing its usual tricks, had shut off the electricity throughout the building. We lit matches, climbed up to the attic, and penetrated the gloom of the studio.

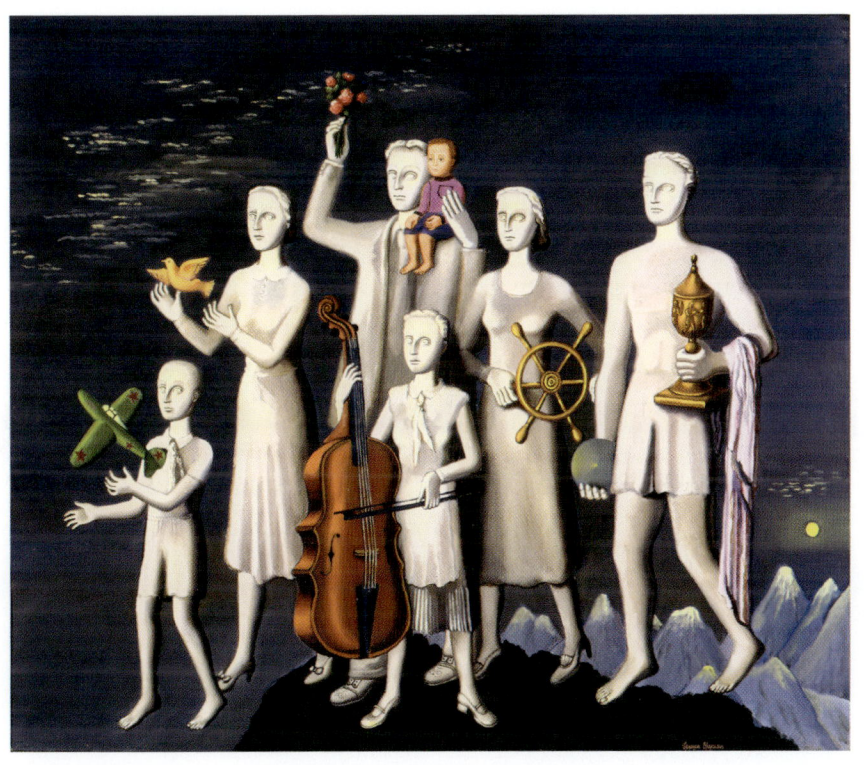

Grisha Bruskin, *Memorial*, oil on linen.

By Candlelight

With my paintings lit by candlelight, I showed the Parisians *Fundamental Lexicon*.

There was no reaction. The guests were utterly indifferent to what they were seeing.

The next day, in daylight, Alesya took an iron and tried without success to remove the candle wax that had dripped onto the painting.

When she met Alvarez at the Sotheby auction, she showed him the "birthmarks" from that memorable evening.

A few days later, the businessman once again appeared at the studio, asking me to sell him something as an old friend.

I refused.

Two years later, Alvarez felt that his moment had come. He sold his collection at one of the New York auction houses.

Apogee

The apogee of the commotion that had begun to surround Soviet nonconformist art was the auction of Russian avant-garde and contemporary Russian art held by Sotheby's in Moscow.

In the USSR, the state maintained a monopoly on art. There was no art market whatsoever.

The entire country could boast of five or six collectors with an interest in nonconformist artists. The latter, as a rule, gave them their paintings as gifts.

The words "gallery" and "auction" were not in use.

We had an incredibly primitive understanding of the art world in the West.

An artist acquaintance of mine, showing me a contemporary art catalog from Sotheby's, informed me that to turn up on the pages of a publication like that was a sign of international renown.

The participants in the Moscow auction regarded the impending event with trepidation.

A Personal Decision

The initiator of the event was the superb connoisseur of modern art, Simon de Pury. The head of Sotheby's European division, he was also the curator of the collection of Baron von Tissen.

Simon made the rounds of artist studios in Moscow. He got to know the European collections of Russian underground art. He studied the essays and monographs published on the subject in the West.

He put together a list of artists and presented it to the Ministry of Culture.

Under pressure from the Ministry, the auctioneers agreed to include a few official artists.

I was represented by six paintings, including *Fundamental Lexicon*, for which it was necessary to get the personal permission of the new Minister of Culture.

His underlings utterly refused to take the responsibility, explaining in private conversations that if they did so they might lose their jobs and leave their wives and little children at risk of starvation.

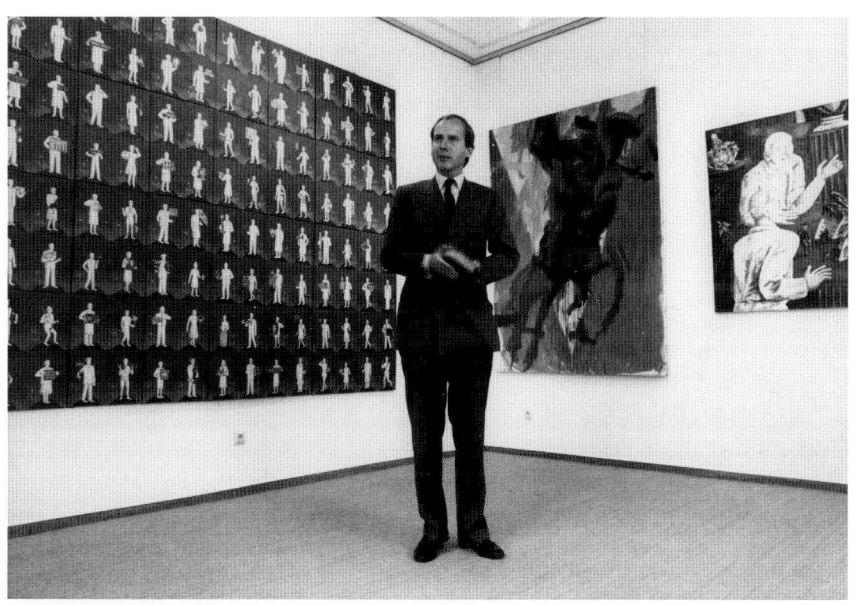

Simon de Pury in front of Grisha Bruskin's painting *Fundamental Lexicon*,
on the eve of the Sotheby Moscow auction, 1988.
Photograph by Klaus Meyer-Anderson.

A Cultural Safari

The timing for the upcoming event was most propitious.

On the one hand, prices in the Western art market had reached their height on the eve of a recession, while on the other, a captivated world was following Gorbachev's initiatives with delight and hope.

The auction had been skillfully advertised.

Sotheby's had organized exhibitions in Western art capitals—New York, London, Paris, and Cologne—accompanying them with lectures by critics and scholars.

Prospective collectors had an interesting itinerary planned for them in Russia.

They had been guaranteed the right to export their purchases to the West unhindered and duty-free.

It was a kind of cultural safari.

Russian aborigines were not to be found in the ranks of potential buyers, since the country didn't have any collectors with money.

Payment was to be in hard currency, the possession of which by a Soviet citizen was a criminal act.

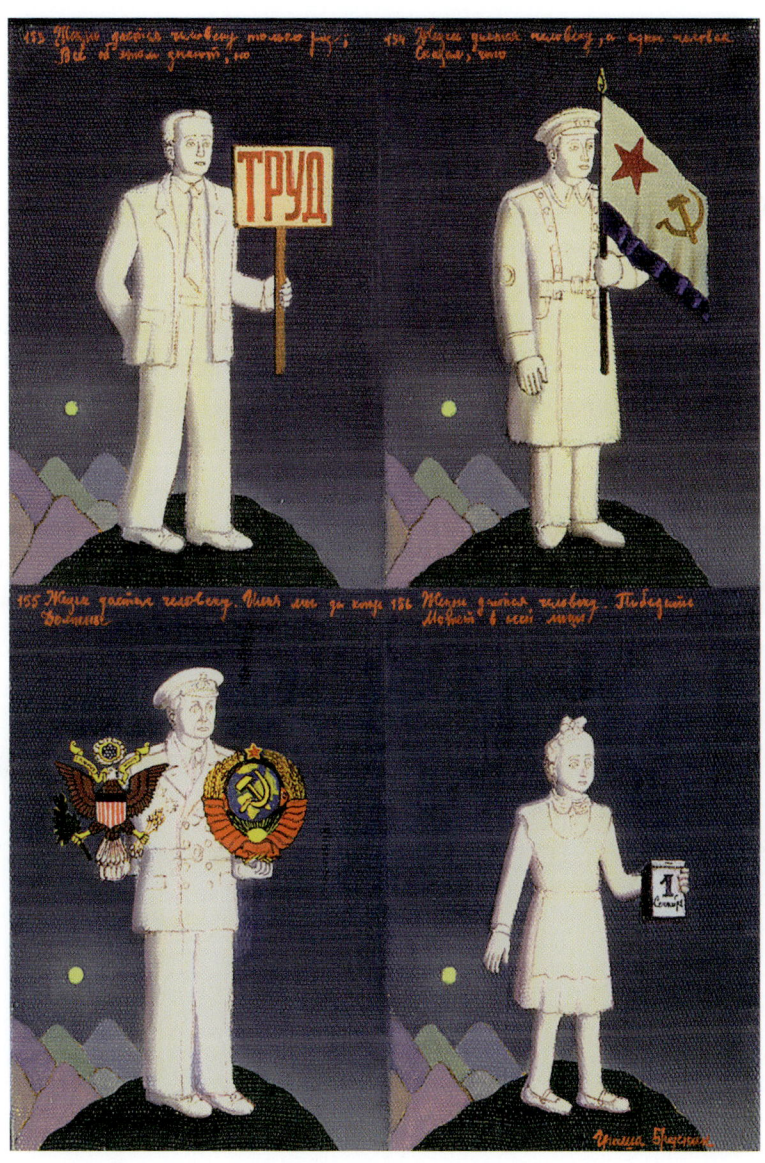

Grisha Bruskin, *Fundamental Lexicon* (fragment), oil on linen.

Heaven on Soviet Earth

The attention of the foreign press was directed to the Hammer Center in Moscow, where the auction was to take place.

The center had been built by Armand Hammer, the American friend of the eternally living Lenin.

It was a rather strange institution. Police guarded it from infiltration by ordinary Soviets, whose presence there was categorically forbidden.

Crossing the threshold, the lucky visitor was catapulted from the poor, gray, deficit-ridden Soviet reality into a magical heavenly oasis of Western abundance.

Inside the building towered an artificial tree of astonishing proportions, no doubt the tree of the knowledge of good and evil. Around the tree were elegant restaurants, expensive designer boutiques, and offices of Western businessmen.

Payment in this heaven on Soviet earth was exclusively in hard currency.

The Creeps Want Hard Currency

For the catalog cover and the poster, Sotheby's chose *Fundamental Lexicon*.

This induced the predictable ire of the Ministry of Culture.

The organizers of the sale had promised the artists 60 percent of the proceeds, to be paid as an honorarium.

The authorities had not permitted direct contact between the participants and the auction house. Instead, we were expected to sign a contract with the Ministry of Culture.

Imagine our surprise when, two days before the event, we were invited to the Ministry of Culture to sign papers from which the aforementioned 60 percent had disappeared without a trace.

The artists unanimously said *nyet*, intimating that we might remove our works from the auction.

They argued with us, they tried misleading us. We were threatened.

Finally, one exasperated Ministry lady screamed:

"There's no bread in the country, people are living on 150 rubles a month, and you creeps want hard currency."

The artists replied firmly:

"We do."

In the end, the authorities backed down. The contract was signed.

Bread and Salt

A week before the event, Western collectors began a series of organized visits to the studios of participating artists.

Just in time, the studios were supplied with food and drink. The government wanted to show off the standard of living among Soviet citizen-artists, at the same time engaging the Russian tradition of bread and salt.

Transformed into waiters, KGB agents served the guests.

Every day, Western journalists and TV crews with cameras interviewed us.

On the Eve

The day before the sale, there was a cocktail party and elegant candlelight dinner at the Hammer Center.

Wealthy foreign visitors, including some with royal titles, were dressed to the nines. Glamorous ladies appeared in evening gowns and jewels. Men were in tuxedos or expensive suits.

The artists in their Czech pants and Polish shirts looked like poor relations.

All around people whispered and smiled enigmatically. Mysterious vapors hung in the air.

An employee of the auction house walked up to me and said in my ear:

"Grisha, I don't have the right to say this, but tomorrow your *Fundamental Lexicon* is going to sell for crazy money. I have a bid for $20,000."

The owner of Sotheby's, Taubman, had apparently said that he'd never seen anything like my paintings and that these were the icons of our century.

I was approached by mysterious representatives, the envoys of foreign eminences.

Several people, introducing themselves, informed me that they had come to Moscow to buy my works. One charming elderly lady, sitting next to me at dinner, bet me a bottle of French cognac that tomorrow *Lexicon* would sell for $100,000. The scene was getting tense.

I had the feeling that I had landed in an Agatha Christie movie in which I was to be the villain.

In White Gloves

The auction took place on July 7, 1988.

It was held in the huge auditorium of the Hammer Center.

Dozens of cameras and video cameras documented the proceedings.

Russian observers present at the events were surprised by the swiftness of their unfolding.

Competing buyers placed their bids. Those who were in the auditorium held up cards with numbers on them. Those who were in other countries called in on numerous telephones scattered throughout the hall.

On the electronic board that reflected the course of the sale, numbers replaced one another with exceptional speed.

The artists felt like athletes, slugging it out in an open arena.

The auction was brilliantly conducted by the elegant Simon de Pury.

Sotheby workers in white gloves carried to the stage the canvases of nonconformist artists that just a few days back had been gathering dust in cramped studios.

In Addition to Its Bears and Red Commissars

The auction was phenomenally successful.

The majority of works were sold for prices far exceeding the opening bids.

The West suddenly discovered that this far-off, incomprehensible northern country boasted, in addition to its bears and red commissars, a free and original art. Which was distinguished not only from profane socialist realism but also from contemporary European and American art.

And that this art, like the art of the early Russian avant-garde, could enrich the cultural history of western civilization.

There were a few failures.

The hall burst into applause every time the bids for the painting of some well-known Kremlin artist, foisted on Sotheby's by the government, failed to reach the price shown in the catalog.

The Crime

My six paintings sold for 503,800 pounds sterling ($930,000 at the time), which amounted to seven, six, three, nine, fourteen, and seventeen times their respective starting prices.

The painting called *Memorials* was acquired by a major collector of contemporary art from Switzerland. *Monuments* ended up in a different Swiss collection. *The Partner* became part of a French collection. *Alefbet No. 15* was bought by a collector from Long Island, who at the same auction acquired paintings by Rodchenko and Stepanova. The diptych *Alefbet No. 3, No. 4* ended up with a collector from Canada.

The greatest success was *Fundamental Lexicon,* which sold for 242,000 pounds ($416,000).

Immediately after the auction my family started kissing and congratulating me. They were joined by a few friends (the ranks of the latter having suddenly shrunk), as well as by foreigners known and unknown who asked for autographs and interviews.

Bureaucrats from the Ministry of Culture were walking past with stony faces, trying not to look in my direction.

The crime had been committed.

Incognito

In the middle of everything, one of the organizers came up to me and told me in confidence that the anonymous purchaser of *Fundamental Lexicon* wanted to meet with me.

We immediately set off for the hotel, which was located right there in the Hammer Center, and knocked at the door.

We were met by an elderly couple.

The man said his name. He was a well-known German collector from Bavaria.

He said that he and his lady companion had first seen the painting on exhibition in Cologne and had traveled to Moscow in order to buy it.

Later I found out that the main competitor of this Bavarian Incognito was the English musician Elton John.

The next day, carried away, he asked Sotheby's to relay to the German collector his proposal to buy *Fundamental Lexicon* at a higher price than it had sold for the previous day.

The German refused.

Take It Just in Case

Never in my life had I found money.

Late at night after the auction, on our way home from the Hammer Center, my wife and I found five rubles on the street.

Alesya asked me:

"Should we pick it up or are we already rich?"

I answered:

"Take it just in case."

I was right. I understood that the Soviet State would think up some way to appropriate such a large sum of money.

The next morning I brought to the Hammer Center Hotel the bottle of French cognac I had bet on the night before.

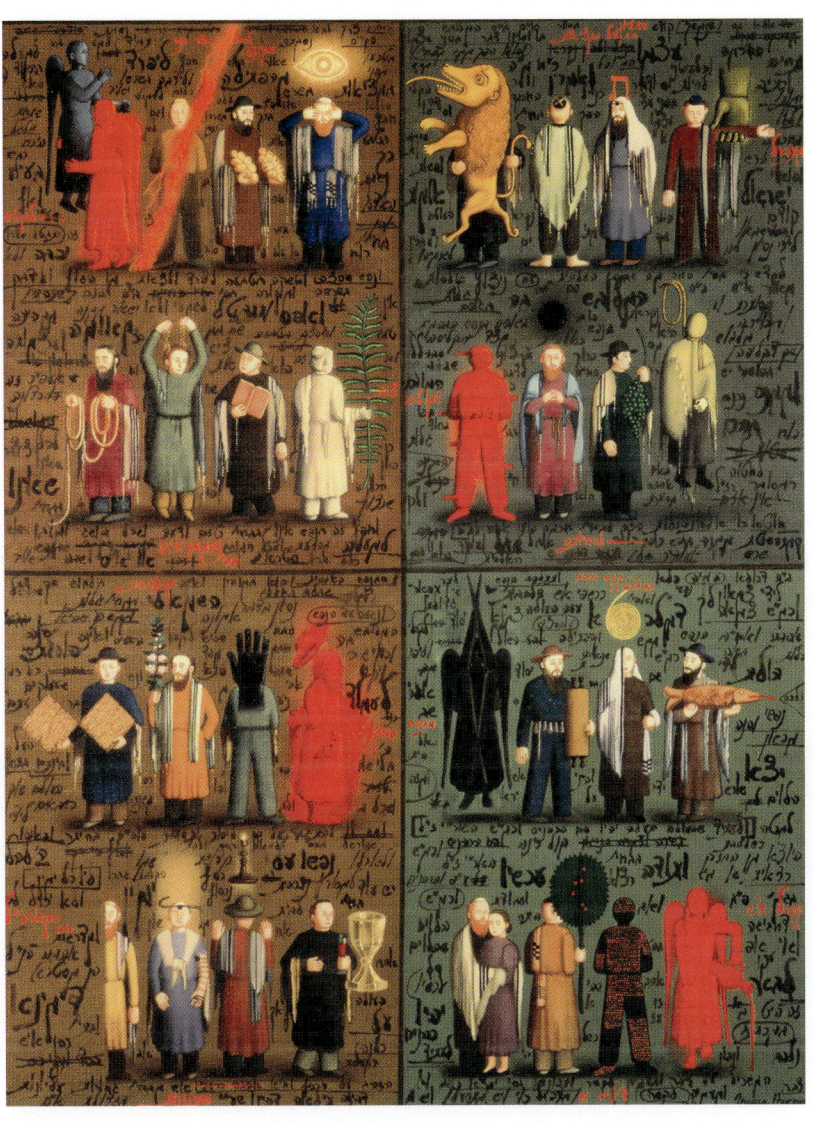

Grisha Bruskin, *Alefbet*, oil on linen.

A Young Man with a Pleasant Face

That same day, the artists organized a cruise on the Moscow River, inviting the foreign guests.

A young man with a pleasant face came up to me.

He said that he had tried to buy *The Partner* at the auction but had been outbid. He also said that he wrote for the American magazine *ArtForum*, and was working on a book.

Later, the writer put together a book about Moscow unofficial art. Rhapsodizing on the beautiful Roman profiles of Russian artists and the aristocratic femmes fatales with the features of Greta Garbo and the hearts of Joan of Arc, he did not forget me.

I appeared as an ugly dwarf, a "tiny, gnarled, nervous man," and in the magazine version, a "tiny Jew." The word "Jew," as politically incorrect in the given context, was later excised, apparently by the publisher.

The young man with a pleasant face, opening the eyes of the world, declared that all my life I had been an official artist of mediocre talent but had my nose to the wind, and as soon as the danger had passed I seized the moment and moved to the opposite camp.

Possessed of an empty soul, I deceived the West, blinding world opinion to the existence of the "genuine, original" artists of the Russian underground.

P.S. My wife, Alesya, insists that I insert my photograph exactly here.

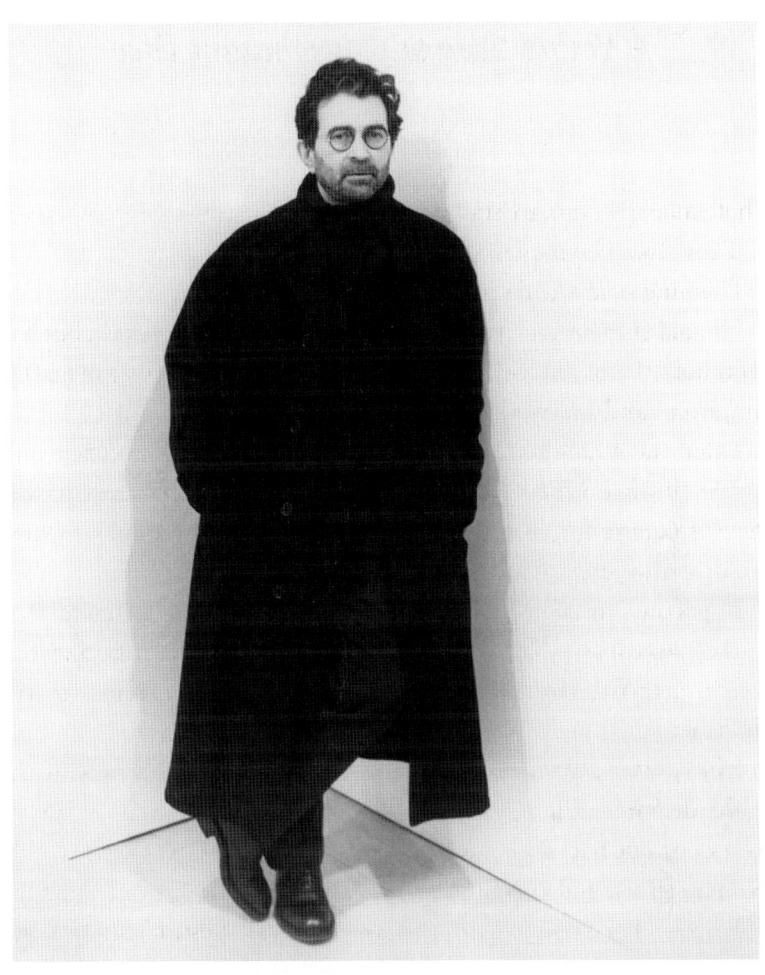

In New York, 1996.
Photograph by Marianna Volkov.

A *Zionist Conspiracy*

The auction inflamed people's imaginations.

They started fantasizing. Rumors flew.

I heard that the Sotheby auction was a Zionist conspiracy, intended to denigrate "genuine" Russian art. On this account I was called to the Ministry of Culture.

People said that the government of Israel had bought up all my paintings (instead of spending the money on defense).

They said that I had an uncle who lived in Canada or maybe in America, and who, instead of buying the paintings cheaply from me at the studio, spent a million to get it at the auction.

In the version of one artist, all my paintings had been acquired by a jewelry company. Embittered, apparently, by the fact that they had bought my paintings and not his, the great man threatened to start a law suit against me and the mythic company.

In his words, ever since the auction he had been living with an "unhealed wound."

It was said that all the works went to rich Brooklyn Jews.

A more original version was put forward by a gallery owner from Soho, who informed his listeners that the sale of my paintings was the work of U.S. intelligence. Desiring to support oppositional organizations in the USSR, the CIA had used the auction to get money into Russia.

"A dirty story," he concluded.

A gallery owner in Pittsburgh who was involved in Russian art took a different route. She took the selling price of *Fundamental Lexicon*, divided by 128 (the number of figures depicted there), and concluded that the price for each figure was extremely modest.

As she saw it, it wasn't a success, but a failure.

When I returned to Moscow ten years later, I heard from an attractive, well-known Moscow gallery owner that as an insider she knew beyond a doubt that there had been a conspiracy of Western galleries. The dealers, apparently, had come to Moscow earlier and bought up paintings of participating artists while they were cheap. Then, at the auction, they paid astronomical sums so that, in the future, they could raise the prices on the works of those artists.

That's the way they do things in the West, she declared.

I had the feeling I was talking to a KGB agent for disinformation.

You're Still Young, You'll Get Your Chance

In 1988, John Wilson, the president of the Chicago International Art Exposition invited me, on the recommendation of Bill Struve, to come to Chicago and make the poster for this event.

With this goal in mind, he included me in the cultural exchange program he had organized between the United States and the USSR.

Three American artists were to spend some time working in Russia, and three Russians were to come to the United States.

A few months before the Moscow auction, I received a copy of the official invitation, made out in my name and sent by Wilson to the Artists Union of the USSR.

Telephoning the International Department of the Artists Union, I found out that, indeed, an official invitation in my name had been received.

At the same time, I was informed that lots of artists wanted to travel to Chicago, and that there was a line, in which I occupied last place.

"It's all right," said the head of the Department. "You're still young, you'll get your chance."

I said something rude, hung up, and tried to forget the whole business.

Speaking Politely for the First Time

Ten days before the Sotheby auction that same official called me up and, speaking politely for the first time, said:

"Listen, Bruskin. Two weeks from now you're going to Chicago. Why haven't you filled out the forms?"

I understood that the cultural policies and overall mission of the Artists Union were undergoing a change.

Inspired, I ran around collecting signatures.

I had to get a whole set of forms and approvals, including the approval of the Party Organization of the Moscow Section of the Artists Union, affirming my political reliability and moral probity.

It was my duty not to disgrace the country.

I have to say that not so long before this organization had regarded me as an amoral individual, an antisocial element, a dangerous, covert enemy of the bright Communist Tomorrow and Today.

My experience with the Party organization was the same as with the Artists Union.

At first they informed me that the Union included many artists much superior to me, and that someone of my mediocre abilities could not possibly go abroad as the representative of the truest art in the world.

You're Coming with Me, Comrade

A few days later, for reasons unknown to me, the authorities changed their minds and permitted the trip.

Up to the last minute I expected a "gentleman in civilian clothes" to walk up to me in the airport and say:

"You're coming with me, Comrade."

I left for the United States five days after the Moscow auction.

Over the Hills and Far into America

At the height of summer, two colleagues and I flew to Chicago.

John Wilson and Bill Struve met me at the airport.

Wilson, seizing the moment, took me aside and, assuming that I had just emerged from the stone age in the Siberian taiga, said:

"A bad situation, old man, you're being followed by the KGB and the FBI. There are agents everywhere. Hold on to me, I'll protect you."

Bill's attempt to invite me to his house resulted in an altercation.

Wilson, imagining that I was his valuable and legitimate property, had taken me to his "creative retreat" over the hills and far away in the wilds of Michigan.

The weather didn't exactly smile on us. There was a tropical heat wave. One step outside and I understood that the local climate was lethal to the Russian-born.

Despite what seemed to be a decent literary knowledge of the country, I was on an alien planet.

I could speak English all right, but the only person I understood was Bill Struve, who in a previous life must have been an English teacher, and apparently a remarkable one.

Exhausted morally and physically, I felt miserable.

The Uncensored American Telephone Network

My plans were to produce the promised lithograph for the poster and check out the possibilities for a sculpture project that was important to me.

When I got to the retreat, I understood that there was nothing whatsoever for me to do there. Instead of a lithograph stone, I was shown a nice little room with an impressive number of neatly arranged virgin canvases, which I was apparently supposed to transform into artistic masterpieces for my protector from life-threatening surveillance.

The next day, in a solemn and noble gesture, the boss handed each of us thirty dollars and drove us in an organized fashion to that wonder of wonders, the shopping mall, to buy summer clothes.

It turned out that my room did not have direct access to the uncensored American telephone network. Trying to talk with friends from New York or Chicago, I kept hitting an impenetrable wall. Even when I managed to break through, the calls could be terminated at any moment at the whim of the "operators."

Everywhere I went, I was accompanied by a pair of nice girls, the boss's employees.

Salvation

Three days later I got up at five A.M., put a quarter in my pocket, and set out on the American road in search of a phone booth.

A few kilometers later, in the middle of nowhere, I found the desired object. I called Bill Struve and asked to be kidnapped.

Without warning Wilson, Bill came for me with two cars and three big guys. I had prepared my bags in advance. Now I jumped into the car, and we headed for Chicago.

At long last in the free city of Chicago, I moved in with Bill and Deborah Struve and started working enthusiastically in a lithography studio.

Further contacts with my unsuccessful jailer were carried out exclusively through Bill or a lawyer.

When the lithograph was done, I gave Wilson the number of copies specified in the contract and he, using my lithograph, printed the poster for the Chicago International Art Exposition of 1988.

Beautiful Green Swimming Trunks

Arriving in America right after the auction, I discovered my paintings and my own self on the covers and inside pages of numerous magazines and newspapers, including the *New York Times*.

The Chicago art establishment was intrigued by this unusual overseas traveler.

I started getting invitations.

One day, Bill called my studio and said that a well-known Chicago collector, who owned my works, was inviting us to a lunch in my honor.

Warning me that a dip in the collector's swimming pool would be part of the event, he picked me up in his car.

I didn't have anything to swim in, so we went to Bloomingdale's.

I chose a very beautiful pair of green trunks.

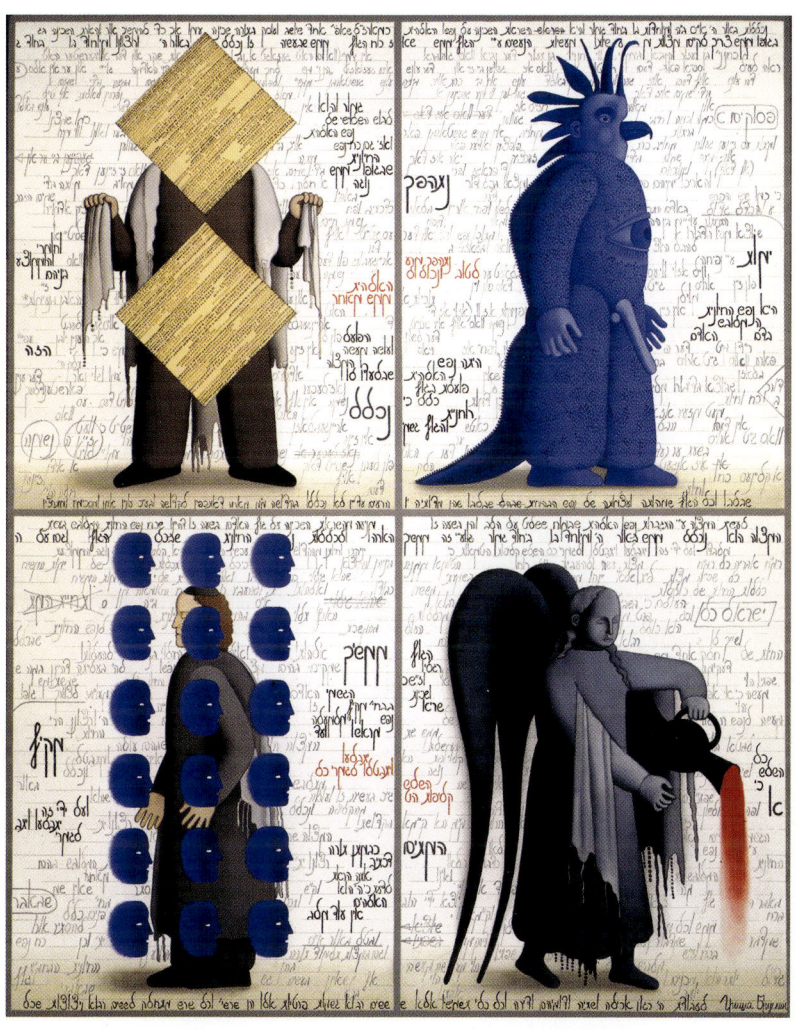

Grisha Bruskin, *Message,* oil on linen.

267

The Highlight

The collector greeted us warmly.

He showed us his architectural treasure with its magnificent collection of paintings and took us out to a dazzling pool.

Around the pool were little tables set for the coming feast.

The weather was splendid.

The guests who had already gathered seemed exceptionally beautiful, intelligent, and kind.

Everybody made a beeline for me.

One lady compared my emigration from Communist Russia to capitalist America with her own move from Los Angeles to Chicago. Another asked whether the Berlin Wall was still standing in Red Square, and if so how I felt about it.

The food was uniformly excellent. Waiters in white tuxedos passed silently among the tables.

I felt like the highlight of the program.

What It Means to Be an Artist in Russia

It was time for a swim.

I set off for the bathroom and put on my newly acquired trunks.

The pool was an Olympic type, with a diving board suspended over the transparent water.

I decided to dive.

Standing on the diving board, I noticed that the eyes of everyone present were fixed on the enigmatic newcomer: me.

I remembered my athletic childhood, leaped up, and like a beautiful fish flew at an angle straight into the water.

Once there, I nearly had a heart attack: the treacherous trunks with their hidden and hence untied drawstring had also taken flight, in precisely the opposite direction.

Reborn in the sea foam, I relied on will power to take myself in hand. Sparkling from behind, trying not to let my embarrassment show (everything's under control here!) I finally caught the floating trunks and managed to get myself into them.

Neither dead nor alive, I returned to the party.

To my astonishment, my popularity had increased significantly.

The guests, particularly of the female variety, literally didn't leave me alone and plied me with questions.

For example, what does it mean to be an artist in Russia?

A Feeling of Guilt

In Russia, I always had to feel guilty.

For being born a Jew. For dressing differently from other people. For reading the wrong books. For never saying "us." For wanting to see the world.

For becoming an artist and then creating the wrong kind of art.

In America it turned out that I wasn't guilty of anything.

Cigarettes with a Similar Name

My first days in New York I stayed in the studio of a friend of mine on Broadway, in Soho.

On the subject of New York galleries I knew absolutely zero.

Pretty soon I got a call from the New York division of Sotheby's. They said there was a collector who wanted to meet me.

Flying in from a suburban mansion in his private jet, the collector arrived at my studio.

When he had introduced himself, he told me that he would like to help me find a gallery. He named, as I now know, a few of the best in New York.

I picked Marlborough because at the time I was smoking cigarettes with a similar name.

The Gold Key

A few days later I was introduced to the director of the Marlborough Gallery in New York, Pierre Levy.

I showed him my work, and we agreed to collaborate.

Time passed, and nobody appeared with a contract. Responses to my telephone calls were polite and vague. I decided to forget about it.

Suddenly the gallery called with the information that Mr. Frank Lloyd was in the city and wanted to see my work.

At the appointed time, a smallish gentleman with a welcoming smile walked into the studio: the legendary art dealer.

He looked over the paintings, smiled, and said:

"I don't know how the American public is going to react to your work. But this I'll say: I've been involved in art all my life and have never seen anything like this."

The next day I got another call from Marlborough telling me to come with a lawyer and sign a contract.

I understood whose gold key had opened that magic door.

Who Was a Crook, and Who Wasn't

Bill Struve took me to the Tallix foundry in upstate New York.

I started work on the sculpture group *Birth of a Hero*.

The task was to sculpt and cast fifteen monumental figures in stainless steel.

I found myself in an unfamiliar reality.

It was hard to make sense of the technological process and business arrangements, and hard to figure out who was a con man and who wasn't.

Reality forced me to cope.

Capitalist Production

The sculptures of *Birth of a Hero* were intended as the central work of the exhibition planned for the Marlborough Gallery.

As I worked, I discovered that Soviet conceptions of capitalist production and ethics were highly idealized.

Dick Polich, the owner of Tallix, took on an enormous number of orders, missed his deadlines, and finished his work in a hurry, doing his best to cut corners.

This looked a lot like the frenzy preceding big Communist holidays. I became anxious and ill.

Shining Visitors

Finally, after a year and a half of work, two days before the opening, the project was finished.

The sculptures were loaded onto huge trucks and the cortege set off for New York.

That night, a crane hoisted the shining visitors onto the open terrace of the gallery, on the second floor of the building on Fifty-seventh Street.

The exhibition opened on time.

The City Retreated

A few years later, I showed *Birth of a Hero* in the Alex Meyerovich Gallery in San Francisco.

Right before that, Rodney King had been beaten up by police in Los Angeles. There were race riots.

Passions were inflamed.

In San Francisco, crowds armed with whatever they could find went from store to store, destroying everything in their path.

The city retreated.

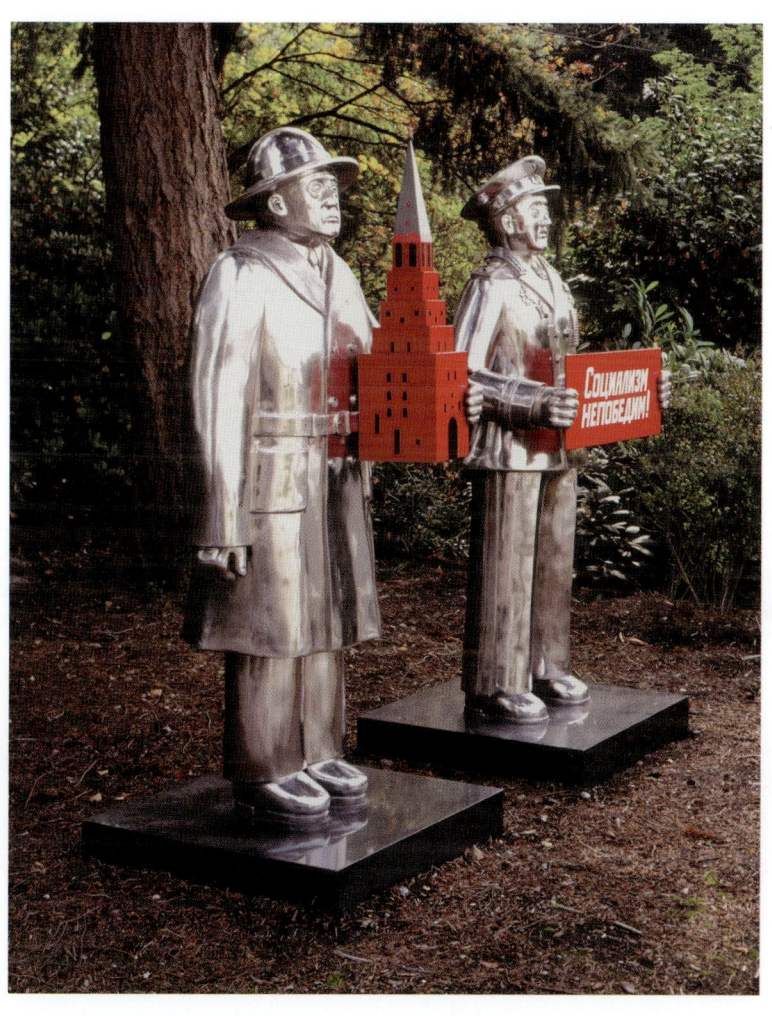

Grisha Bruskin, from the series *Birth of a Hero*,
stainless steel, industrial enamel.

Art Touched the Masses

After ransacking the neighboring Fila sportswear store, the mob moved on to the Meyerovich Gallery.

Alex, full of anxiety, observed the proceedings from the window of a building across the street.

In that gallery were paintings by Picasso and Matisse, Lichtenstein and Warhol.

The mob reached the gallery windows and stopped dead.

Staring at them, resplendent, were Soviet ideological monsters.

Seized by an atavistic fear, the rioters spent a few moments in mute paralysis and then moved on, smashing the windows of the store next door.

Art had successfully touched the masses.

Meyerovich thanked his lucky fate—and also me.

What's in a Versace?

My friends wanted to show me a good time and took me to Brighton Beach.

To my astonishment, I found myself among people I had never seen in Russia. Along the streets strolled men whose hairy chests were draped with weighty Stars of David. Women wore leopard pants and gold open-toed shoes.

A grocery store sold Russian "Belochka" chocolates, Russian "Dymok" cigarettes, and an enigmatic "Versace" cake.

A customer walked up to the counter.

"What's in a Versace?"

The saleswoman yelled to someone in the back:

"Sasha, what's in a Versace?"

The invisible Sasha:

"What do you mean, what's in a Versace? How should I know? Chocolate, nuts."

The cashier:

"If you're that excitable, you shouldn't go shopping."

The customer:

"What else is there to do?"

Just Ignore It!

Outside two women were talking:
   "The doctor said maybe I'll die and maybe I won't."
   "Oh! Just ignore it!"

An Invitation to Tea

On my birthday, October 21, 1988, the perestroika-minded Soviets allowed my wife to go to Switzerland on a personal invitation.

I flew to Zurich with the idea that we would travel around a bit and return together to New York.

In accordance with procedures then in effect, we were supposed to sign in at the Russian consulate in Berne.

While in Berne, we stayed at the home of a collector, a well-known Swiss politician.

At the consulate we were met by none other than the Soviet consul, a man with the face of an inveterate drunk.

It so happened that our Swiss friend, who knew where we were going, had telephoned the consulate to advise us that in the evening he was hosting an official dinner in my honor.

The telephone call made an impression on the Soviet bureaucrats.

The ambassador of the Soviet Union in Switzerland, who resided nearby, invited us to tea.

A Broken Taboo

The ambassador turned out to be a Russian woman of tanklike build, with a bun on her head. She looked like the popular singer Zykina.

Madame Ambassador spent some time complaining that Switzerland was a difficult country and then inquired about our plans.

I stupidly informed her that we were going to Paris.

"Is Moscow aware of this?" she asked.

The next morning, the drunk consul telephoned us and in a hoarse, hung-over voice asked us to hold off on Paris until he consulted with "certain people."

"With the KGB?" I asked innocently.

"What do you mean, Grigordavydich, why talk like that?" exclaimed the consul.

I had broken a taboo. In ancient times, people couldn't name either the threatening God or the mysterious animal.

The Master's Favorite Subjects

The official dinner had taken place the previous day.

The guests began to arrive.

The first guest I saw was an elegant lady holding a Pekinese.

She was wearing a diamond brooch, the insignia of an imperial maid-of-honor, from the workshop of Fabergé. Something told me that it wasn't from an antique shop.

The stranger turned out to be Varenka Mark, née Princess Urusova, the daughter of a maid-of-honor of the last Russian empress. She later became our dear friend.

After Varenka and her husband, Olivier, came another couple: a very old man and his beautiful Japanese wife.

The old man held out his hand and introduced himself:

"Balthus."

"You mean you're still alive?" I came perilously close to asking. I was convinced that the great man had long since died and now belonged to history.

My wife sat next to him at dinner.

Throwing them an occasional glance, I saw that they spent the entire evening in lively conversation.

The next day I started quizzing Alesya impatiently, in the hope of hearing a vivid story about the life and work of the great artist.

It turned out that on this occasion the master had limited himself to two subjects: his recent knee operation and his beloved Chinese chef.

Those Bonaparte Upstarts

We were dining at home with Varenka and Olivier.

Varenka leaned across the table towards Alesya.

"Imagine, darling, Pyotr got divorced!"

"Pyotr who?" asked Alesya, puzzled.

"Why, Pyotr! My cousin, Pyotr Sheremetev. I always knew that the marriage wouldn't last. Of course, Pyotr is no angel, this is obvious. But his wife, Pauline Bonaparte, only married him for his name."

Varenka was right.

If you think about it, who are those Bonaparte upstarts compared to the old Russian aristocracy?

Uncle Konstantin

Varenka continued.

"My uncle Konstantin spent his whole life in Soviet camps. And his tutor waited for him all that time. Then one day my uncle invented something having to do with bees. And because of these wasps he was set free.

"He lived with his tutor right near the Bolshoi Theater and kept asking me to bring him sugar. I'd bring him sugar from Paris. It turned out they were making jam.

"Then he was moved to a faraway neighborhood. Terribly far.

"You had to take the subway and then a bus and then walk.

"But my uncle met us at the bus stop and recited Baudelaire the whole way.

"Somehow, without noticing how, we got there."

In the English Manner

Frank Lloyd invited me to the Bahamas.

My wife and I settled in on the small island of Eleuthera in a spacious and comfortable house, where my work went well.

One day Frank invited us to spend some time in his mansion on neighboring Paradise Island.

Part of the way we went on Lloyd's yacht, piloted by a friendly, intrepid captain dressed all in white.

We were met by an amiable butler, an aging black man, Mr. Johnson.

We followed him into the house, along a special carpeted path.

In everything you could sense an ideal of order.

The estate had an unfathomable number of servants, dressed in spotless uniforms and trained in the English manner. They were hired from the local population.

On our way we passed a man with a net, carefully removing rose petals from the water of a pool.

Another man with gardening shears was trimming the trunks of palm trees.

Big Boobs

The estate was on the ocean.

We were not the only guests.

The next day, everyone went down to the beach and into the water, not far from shore.

Two beautiful girls walked over from the neighboring Club Med. They were topless.

I kept swimming, convinced that either nobody cared or they were pretending not to notice, like characters from English anecdotes popular in Russia.

Suddenly I saw that all the men, including the elderly Lloyd, had stopped swimming, and were staring immobile at the wondrous sight.

"Big boobs," said the old man in a businesslike fashion as I, swimming alone, caught up with him.

The Only Time

Pierre Levy had begun his career as an ordinary assistant in the gallery of his uncle, Frank Lloyd.

One day a man called, gave his name, and asked for Mr. Lloyd.

The connection was poor. Pierre didn't catch the name, and, a little annoyed, asked the called to spell it.

The caller spelled: "P I C A S S O."

That was the only time the future gallery owner spoke with the great master.

According to Custom

Toward the end of his life, the famous sculptor Jacques Lipschitz returned to his religious roots. He became close to the Lubavitcher rebbe.

He died while traveling, in a small town on the island of Capri.

Lloyd called his nephew and asked him to go to Capri and bury the artist in the Holy Land, according to his wishes.

It was one hundred degrees out.

Before the ship departed for Israel, the body had to be kept somewhere.

There was neither a morgue nor a hospital nearby.

Desperate, Pierre turned to the local monastery.

After an impressive contribution to the needs of the monastery, the monks agreed to give the departed man a temporary refuge.

In the building where they brought the body hung a cross. When she saw that, the widow exclaimed that lying under a cross, the dead man would turn in his grave.

For an additional sum, the Christian symbol was removed.

A few days later, a ship took the artist's body to the shores of the Promised Land.

Jacques Lipschitz was buried according to Jewish custom.

The Working Name

My wife stopped by the business office of the Marlborough Gallery.
On the office wall she noticed a list of the gallery's artists.
Next to each name was the name of the artist's wife.
Alesya started reading:
Red Grooms—Lucy
Manolo Valdes—Rosa
Grisha Bruskin—Aleksandra
Alex Katz—Ada
When she reached Larry Rivers, she found a long list of crossed-out wives.
At the end, in fresh ink, appeared the final, working name.

The Primorsky Restaurant

One day, Pierre Levy said:

"Grisha, take me to Brighton Beach, I've heard so much about it."

It was a weekday. I reserved a table at the Primorsky Restaurant.

The food was fried. It was greasy and not very good. Fat waitresses in miniskirts knocked into tables.

To the question, "what wines do you have?" we received not a list, but a retort:

"What kind could we have? White or red."

On stage, Jews impersonated gypsies, badly. Horrific paintings hung on the walls.

In a far corner sat the Mafia-style owner in a Georgian cap, talking endlessly on a cell phone.

Suspicious characters darted in and out.

I felt embarrassed.

Let's Go to Brighton Beach!

Pierre and his wife, Rosie, were enchanted with everything.

They loved the food. They saw the paintings as amusing kitsch. The "gypsies," the owner, and the whole restaurant scene struck them as real life.

The gallery owner gazed at the waitresses with unconcealed pleasure.

Since then, every time we need to get together, Pierre, to my horror, proposes:

"Let's go to Brighton Beach!"

For Bouillon Cubes

I was having dinner with Garry Kasparov.

Kasparov said that he was flying to Baku to save his relatives because in ten days there would be an Armenian pogrom.

The tragedy took place.

Garik arrived in time and flew his family to safety.

Later, at a gathering at a friend's house, I mentioned that the timing of the pogrom was known in advance and that, in all probability, it had been organized by the KGB with the knowledge of Gorbachev, like similar events in Vilnius and Tbilisi.

A Soho artist who was present came over to me. Fingering the cloth of my jacket, she asked, "Where did you buy it?"

Taken aback, I answered "New York."

"You have sold out to the American bourgeoisie," declared the Marxist. "You're making a living by defaming your country."

I remembered the land of my birth, where one sold one's homeland for so much less: some bouillon cubes or a leather jacket, as had been said of the writer Sinyavsky.

She Came on a Visit

At the Flea Market in London, I saw an old woman in a headscarf.

Her worn-out plush jacket and felt boots with galoshes left no doubt about where she was from.

The old women was selling incredible junk: some Soviet copper coins, a dozen commemorative pins, a few random buttons.

My heart contracted. I asked how she had ended up here.

The old lady said that her daughter had married an Englishman. A few years later, she herself had come for a visit. The family didn't get on.

There was no money to return to Russia.

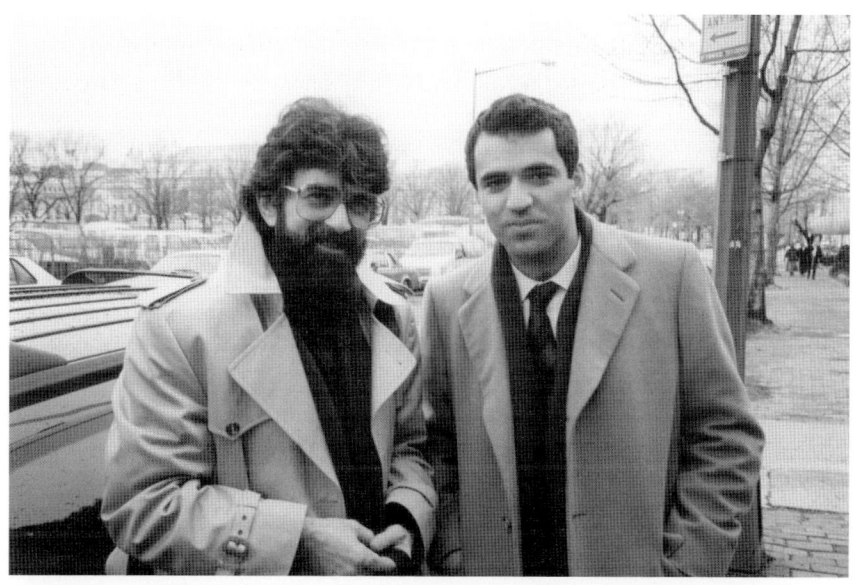

With Garry Kasparov, Washington, 1988.

A Hop, Skip, and a Jump

In Paris, the writer Vladimir Maksimov told me that in the seventies in Australia he had met an old lady just like that.

Maksimov asked her:

"Where are you from, Grandma?"

"From Poltava, Sonny."

"What are you doing here?"

"I came to see my brother."

"Well, and how are things at home, in Poltava?"

"Everybody drinks."

"And your brother?"

"He drinks."

"And where are you going?"

"Home. You go to Singapore, and from there it's a hop, skip, and a jump."

At the Bottom of the Valley of Kedron

When we went to Israel, we met with Misha Shteiglitz, an archeologist who, in the Promised Land, had become a general.

Our friend, who stood six foot five, wore a flannel shirt and jeans and did not mince words.

That night he offered to show us Jerusalem.

The intifada was in full swing.

We emerged from a car on the Mount of Olives and looked, transfixed, down into the valley.

There, in the cemetery at the bottom of the Valley of Kedron, a mysterious ceremony was taking place.

Candles flickered. In the darkness you could make out a white canvas, stretched out to separate the men, dressed in festive embroidered eighteenth-century caftans, white stockings, and fur hats, from the modestly attired women.

You could hear the words of the memorial prayer.

The Shadow

I sensed someone's presence behind my back and turned around.

Along the wall, a man's shadow was creeping towards us. I got anxious and warned Misha.

The general retrieved a gun from his car and stuck it in the back pocket of his jeans.

The gun made an impression. The shadow disappeared.

I asked Misha:

"Would you have shot?"

"If they started throwing stones at us, I wouldn't respond with a bow," he replied calmly.

The Wise Rabbi

In the Israel Museum in Jerusalem, I saw an old rabbi surrounded by young men with sidecurls.

I was surprised that Hasidim could be interested in art.

It turned out that the young men were about to be married.

Their wise teacher had taken them to the museum to show them naked women in classic paintings.

The rabbi felt that seeing the nudes, the bridegrooms would know what to do on their wedding night.

A Hammer on the Knees

It was my turn to get a green card.

For this purpose, at eight A.M. of the appointed day I was to appear at a city clinic.

To prove me worthy of this important document, American doctors had to certify my strapping health.

Awakening in pitch darkness, I quickly dressed and went to the right place at the right time.

In the company of numerous other immigrants, I moved from doctor to doctor, each time patiently waiting to be called.

Then came the neurologist.

The neurologist worked energetically; the line moved fast. Patients were with him maybe three, maybe five minutes.

My turn came. I went into the office.

The doctor commenced an examination that lasted about an hour.

He asked strange questions, looked me in the eye, asked me to stick out my tongue, hold out my hands. And he spent an inordinate amount of time hitting my knees with a little hammer, making my legs kick.

Finally I emerged and took a seat, waiting for the next examination.

Just Like This One

Turning over in my mind why the neurologist had wasted so much precious time on me, I started looking at the shoes of the people seated across from me.

The shoes told detailed and eloquent stories about their owners. Finally, I decided to look at my own shoes through the eyes of those people.

To my astonishment, I discovered that in my haste to get ready I had put on two different shoes: one a brown summer shoe and the other a winter boot in black.

I understood the kind of impression I must be making. The enigma with the neurologist was solved.

I felt like the hero of a popular joke from the seventies.

Brezhnev's retinue was waiting to take him to a meeting.

He walks outside. His secretary says:

"Leonid Ilyich, you're wearing two different shoes."

Brezhnev says: "These are all I have."

The secretary says: "I'm sure you have a pair. Look more closely."

Brezhnev says: "I did look. The other pair is just like this one."

Doctor Winkie

My wife and I went to San Francisco for the opening of my exhibition in the Meyerovich Gallery.

The gallery owner introduced me to a well-known San Francisco collector, Dr. Winkie, a handsome young Chinese man dressed from head to toe in leather and metal.

At the opening I saw the doctor in a different outfit: snow-white sweatpants and sneakers. A bright yellow tuxedo jacket and black tie completed the outfit.

After the banquet, the collector invited us to see his club and restaurant, which he was very proud of. Getting on his motorcycle, he led a procession of cars.

A Valuable Gift

The restaurant was located in a refitted intercontinental jet.

The walls of the billiard parlor next door were decorated with can-vases by Francisco Clemente. The spacious rooms of the discotheque were painted by Keith Harring.

At some point, Dr. Winkie said he wanted to give me a present and took me to his wine cellar.

He cautiously removed a rare old bottle and handed it to me with a meaningful look.

A Momentous Occasion

Anticipating bliss, I kept the valuable gift for a long time, waiting for an appropriately momentous occasion.

One day a bunch of Russians showed up.

We cheerfully drank a lot of vodka. We drank everything there was. We had to get more.

Well under the influence and not thinking clearly, we downed the treasured bottle without noticing its subtle bouquet.

Lady Death

In 1991 in Palm Beach, after a grueling day installing an exhibition in the Grace Hokin Gallery, Alesya and I returned to our hotel.

I proposed going to the hotel bar and having a drink to unwind.

An orchestra was playing. People were dancing.

Suddenly everybody turned around.

Not believing my eyes, I saw Lady Death, scythe in hand.

The Heirs

Stepping uncertainly, leaning on a cane, Death moved through the hall with the help of two playboys sporting California tans.

The hundred-year-old lady was wearing a wig. Her pale, decrepit face was hidden behind dark glasses. What once had been a mouth was covered with bright lipstick.

Her necks, arms, ears, and fashionable short dress from Yves St. Laurent were adorned with diamonds and emeralds.

To our astonishment, the playboys dragged the ruin to the dance floor.

The thought crossed my mind that good-for-nothing heirs had brought the old lady here to dance her to death and come into their phenomenal inheritances.

Propelling the ghost to the music, the "heirs" passionately embraced her, working their hands in unambiguous fashion.

Putting Aside the Bad Dream

The next morning, putting aside the bad dream, we had breakfast in the restaurant.

The waitress told us that the old lady, who had caused a sensation in the hotel, had inherited the incalculable riches of a legendary American oil baron.

She was in fact over a hundred and was known for her unusual erotic exploits.

After a Pause

In 1993, the Pushkin Museum in Moscow held an exhibition of the book project *General Instruction*, a collaboration between me and the poet Lev Rubinshtein.

At the opening, Lev said:

"Either we've really come up in the world, or the museum has sunk really low."

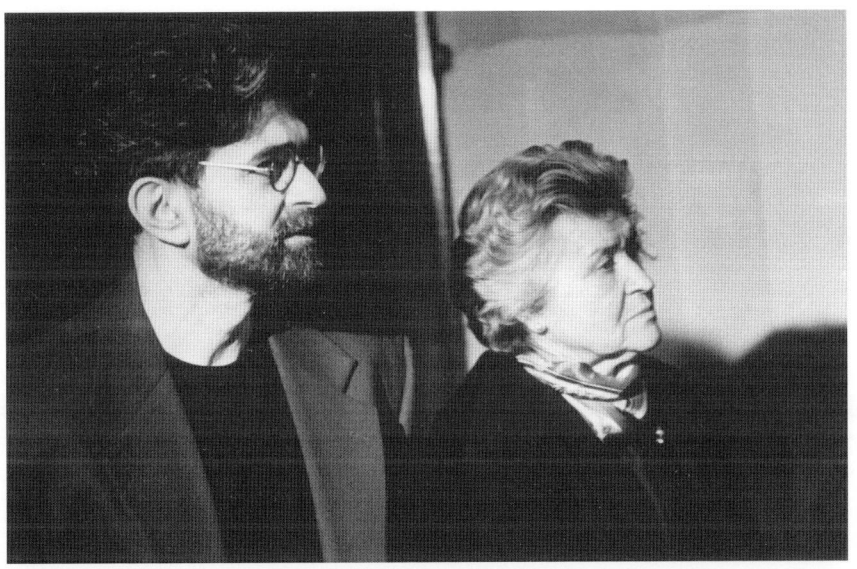

With the director of the Pushkin Museum,
Irina Aleksandrovna Antonovna, 1993.
Photograph by Victor Akhlomov.

The Dearly Beloved Uncle

Our son gave us a puppy.

Rubinshtein, then in New York, said:

"Grisha, I have a big favor to ask of you. Name the dog Moses in honor of my dearly beloved uncle."

I did.

Six months later, I was talking to Lev on the phone and mentioned Moses.

"Who's that?" asked Lev.

"My dog. He was named in honor of your uncle," I reminded him.

"I never had an uncle by that name," said the poet, surprised.

This Is Our Life

Erik Bulatov told us how he painted *Horizon*.

He and Oleg Vasiliev went to the creative retreat in Gurzuf.

The friends were working on illustrations for *Cinderella*, putting together money for a studio.

They smoked a great deal. The room filled with smoke. They opened a window. Erik caught a chill and his back gave out.

The doctor prescribed massage.

During the massage he would lie on his stomach and look out the window at the sea.

The red handrail of the balcony horizontally bisected the landscape, making it hard to contemplate the beautiful view.

For the twentieth time, the artist said to himself:

"This is our life."

And in 1971, he painted *Horizon*.

I've Long Wanted to Make Your Acquaintance

The Bonn Kunsthalle held a big international exhibition called "Europa, Europa," in which I participated.

I went to the opening.

During the opening, I met the poet Prigov. We hadn't seen each other for a long time and stood together chatting.

A pleasant-looking woman walked over to us and, paying no attention to me at all, said in accented Russian to the famous Prigov:

"I recognized you right away! You're the artist Grisha Bruskin! I've long wanted to make your acquaintance!"

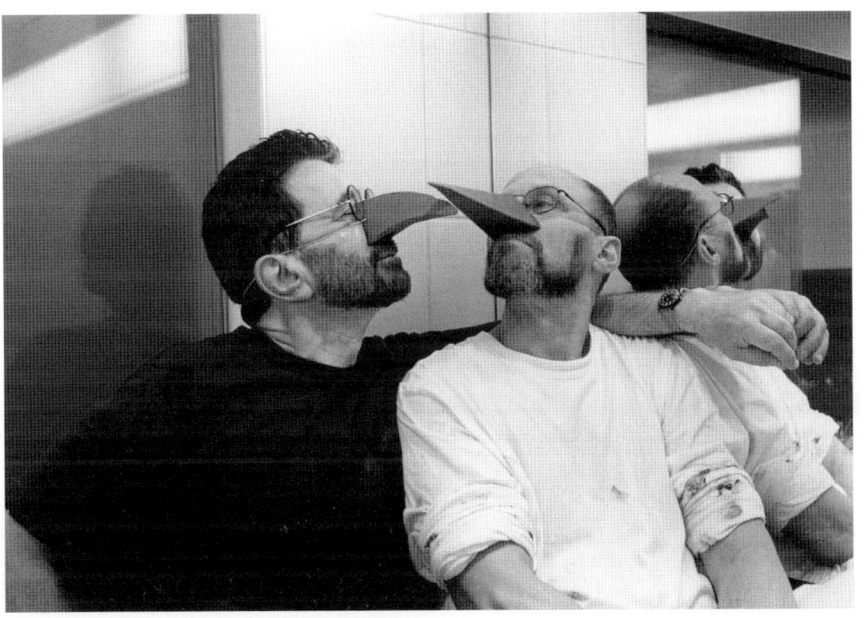

With Dmitry Aleksandrovich Prigov. Performance of
Grisha Bruskin, *Good-bye USSR*, Frankfurt, 2003.
Photograph by Jens Liebchen.

Because I'm an Artist

The artist Volodya Yankilevsky called and asked to borrow a catalog I had.

My wife offered take it over.

Volodya explained that he needed the catalog as part of his application for a green card.

Alesya asked if they had a good lawyer, and how soon he expected to get the vital document.

"In two weeks or so," he answered.

Surprised, Alesya said that it had taken us two years.

Volodya, his head in the clouds, gave her a look full of sympathy.

"You understand, we're in a completely different situation because I'm an artist," he said, apparently assuming that we were seasonal workers.

In the Argentine Pampas

In 1995 I had an exhibition in the National Art Museum of Buenos Aires.

After the opening, the curator of the exhibition, Teresa de Anchorena, invited us to her estate in the Argentine pampas.

An avenue of old trees led to a beautiful old-fashioned house.

An antique car, a carriage, and a hidden garden with sculptures and a fountain completed the mise-en-scene.

Teresa's husband, Carlos, in a red beret and wide Turkish pants gathered at the waist in a broad leather belt and jeweled buckle, pranced around on a first-class horse.

The atmosphere at the candlelit dinner brought to mind the stories of Edgar Allan Poe.

Beautiful Girl

The next day, the carriage set off in the company of a cavalcade of men on horseback. The destination was the neighboring estate whose owner, a well-known architect, was giving a reception in honor of the museum opening.

In the midst of the party, the hostess, Nora, a typical passionate Argentinean, came up to me and said:

"I know a Russian phrase."

"What is it?" I asked.

"Beautiful girl. That's what my mother called me when I was small," explained the Argentinean.

"Let the Ship Pass"

The Russian Samovar restaurant is a well-known spot in New York.

The cream of the Russian emigration gathers here. Stars from Russia make their appearance.

At one point, the singer and fortune-teller Zhenya Shevchenko was working there.

The aging, fat Zhenya would slap her rear end with a tambourine and sing "Let the Ship Pass." Telling fortunes, she'd describe her own past in vivid detail.

Then, letting out an evocative sigh, she'd yell in a deep voice:

"I'm choking! My horses! Away to the steppe!"

Sic Transit

Tyoma and I went to have dinner at the Russian Samovar.

Amazed to see what a man Tyoma had become, the well-educated proprietor gave him a hug and said tenderly, "*Sic transit*, motherfucker!"

The Long-Awaited Contract

I had a close friend in New York named Sasha Edelman.

When I came to America, Sasha was living like a king: a first-rate apartment, a loft in Soho, an office building, a car with a driver, an art collection, a beautiful wife, charming children.

He got tangled up in some risky business and lost everything he had, including his family. His things were sold at auction.

Possessing a quick mind, Sasha thought up various projects with the goal of making not ten thousand, a hundred thousand, or even a million, but thirty or fifty million right away.

Puffing on a cigar, never taking a break, my friend worked twenty hours a day.

Finally he invited me to a restaurant and announced that the next day he would sign the long-awaited contract.

That night Sasha died of a heart attack.

I Say Everything Right Out

The Jewish Museum in New York had an exhibition: "Russian Jewish Artists in a Century of Change, 1890–1990."

On the cover of the catalog was my painting *Monuments*.

One Russian artist, a participant in the exhibition, said:

"You know, old man, I always say everything right out, not behind anyone's back. I really liked the exhibition and the catalog. Frankly, there's only one thing I didn't like."

"What's that?" I inquired.

"The catalog cover."

Pausing for a moment, he finished his thought:

"Well, I could understand if it was Chagall or Levitan. But why you?"

Tsimtsum, *Adam Kadmon, and Sitrei Torah*

An old friend of mine, an artist, called me on the phone.

"Grish, tell me about the holiday Purim. Somebody commissioned a painting. I don't know where to start."

He came over.

"You wouldn't have anything on the Kabbalah, would you? I've always wanted to know what that is."

I gave him Rabbi Philip Berg's *Introduction to Kabbalah.*

Six months later, Alesya and I found ourselves in his studio. He showed us his abstract works from the seventies.

"This is *tsimtsum* and this is Adam Kadmon and these are Sitrei Torah," he said, without missing a beat.

I asked him to return the book.

Later I read in an article by an American art historian that my friend, back in the 1950s, became the first artist to use Jewish mysticism and even theorized about it.

He stood, so to speak, at the source.

Does Your Wife Really Wear Clothes?

A close friend of mine from Lausanne, famous for her collection of contemporary art, held an opening reception for a show in a museum there.

At the party was the artist Jeff Koons. At the time he was married to the famous porno star Cicciolina

He expressed his admiration for the hostess's dress.

"Who made it?" inquired the artist.

"Ungaro," she replied.

"Oh, I'd like to buy my wife something like that!" he said.

"Does your wife really wear clothes?" she asked, surprised.

A Doggy Heart Beating in His Breast

In New York, Jeffrey Daitch was showing Kulik.

On the way to the gallery, we ran into Jeff Koons, who said he was also going to see the naked Russian.

Oleg Kulik, a doggy heart beating in his breast, was running around a metal cage.

With an expressive look, he made it clear that he recognized me.

Oleg's wife, Lyuda Bredikhina, invited me to get closer and greet him. At the bottom of the cage was a little doggy window.

Kulik warmly licked my hand.

An Order

I was standing in front of the Marat Gelman Gallery, talking with friends.

Oleg Kulik walked over.

Lev Rubinshtein warned:

"I'm not referring to anybody in particular. But on the eve of Moscow's 850th anniversary, Luzhkov ordered that all stray dogs should be shot."

A Ditty

A friend of mine in Moscow said he heard a ditty beginning with the words:

"Grisha Bruskin was a Russky . . . "

Unfortunately he forgot how it ended.

You're Married

My friend the artist Vovka Radunsky had a visit from his mother.

Holding her nose, she complained that Vovka's dog Ushik smelled bad.

"It's true," agreed Vovka, "we haven't bathed him in a long time."

"That's not the problem," countered his mother calmly. "He smells because you didn't have him spayed."

There was an argument. Finally Vovka raised an objection:

"But I haven't been spayed. And I don't smell!"

"You're married," snapped his mother.

He Had a Surprise

Vovka bought a car with a remote control.

He went to see some friends and decided to show off a little.

He announced that he had a surprise for everyone.

He called his friends over to the window, intending to operate the car by remote control and make a big impression.

He opened the window.

The air conditioner that had just been installed there fell out and landed on the sidewalk with a great thud, nearly killing two pedestrians.

The unexpected event made Vovka forget about the car.

Everyone thought that was the surprise.

Husband and Wife

Vovka's wife, Jackie, had an old grandmother named Maria Lvovna.

Grandma read the Russian papers. She would cut out articles she particularly liked and mail them to her grandchildren.

Maria Lvovna couldn't live without her television.

When a couple kissed on screen, she was embarrassed.

She'd turn around to the other members of the family and point to the television.

Wanting to explain what had happened, she would say with a smile:

"Husband and wife."

The Guys Weren't Joking

I had to do some remodeling in my New York studio.

Russian builders agreed to do the work inexpensively.

The company was called "Ashot and Sasha Inc." and consisted of two men, Ashot and Sasha.

No sooner did Ashot and Sasha start working when some big black guys appeared and demanded that the Russians hire a representative of their oppressed minority, or else they would make short shrift of them.

Through the window Ashot and Sasha saw a dozen appropriately intimidating thugs with metal chains and decided the guys weren't joking.

The thugs said they would come back in a few days for an answer.

The Official Residence

Two days later, on the wise advice of a friend of mine, Ashot and Sasha told them that the apartment was being prepared for a Russian diplomat.

They gave the telephone number of the Soviet Embassy in Washington. They said that despite racism in Russia, they had a chance of getting work there.

After being thoroughly checked by the KGB, of course.

"The diplomat is with the secret services," they added in a whisper, hinting that the walls were already set up with microphones.

The Russian acronym KGB, along with "sputnik" and "perestroika," was understood everywhere on the planet without translation.

The trusting young thugs got scared and disappeared forever.

Conversations with Brodsky

At someone's party, I met a mournful lady.

People were talking about Solomon Volkov's *Conversations with Brodsky*.

The lady called the book "strange."

I asked her how that strangeness manifested itself.

She said enigmatically:

"Well . . . if you were close to someone . . . "

After a meaningful pause, she gave me her final proof.

"Somehow, I don't remember Joseph saying that."

The most significant moment in the mournful lady's biography was the night she had spent with the drunken genius.

Apparently, on the night in question, she and Joseph had been engaged in other conversations.

The Occupants of 23-A

Solomon Volkov—Monchik—said to me:

"Marianna and I don't see ourselves as Americans or New Yorkers. We see ourselves as the occupants of apartment 23-A."

On another occasion:

"I can write any book on any subject I pick without going outside. I have everything right here."

Monchik never suffers from the urge to leave his apartment.

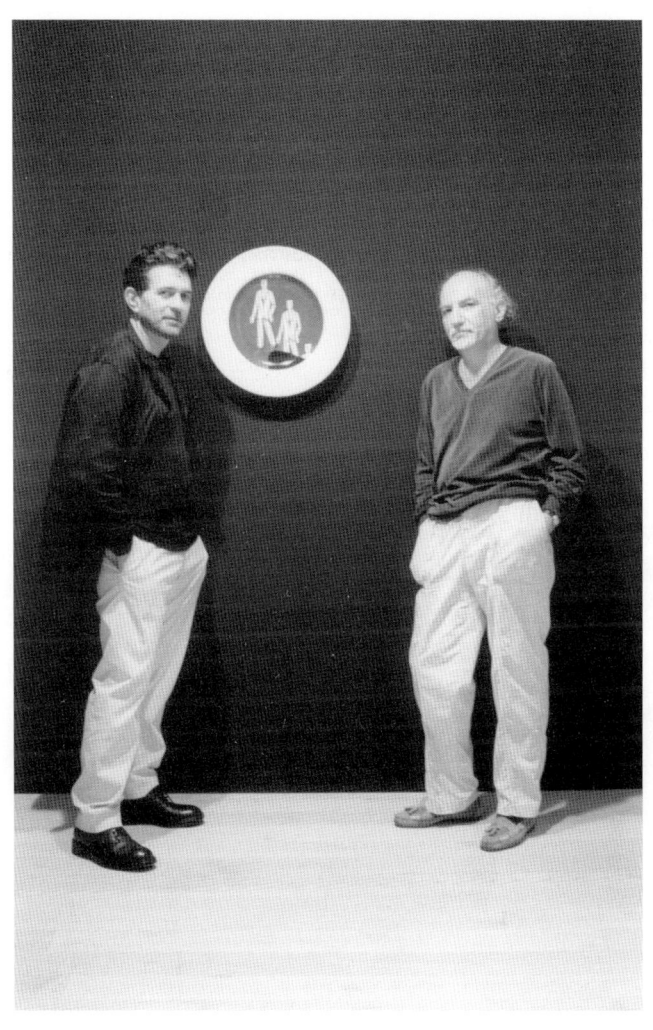

With Solomon Volkov, Marlborough Gallery, 1999.
Photograph by Marianna Volkov.

A Record

One morning I called Marianna and Solomon.

"I hope I didn't tear you away from anything," I told Marianna, knowing full well that she was working day and night preparing a new book of photos for publication.

"What could you tear me away from? Only from cognac," she answered philosophically.

I stopped by to discuss some business.

The next day Monchik called and said:

"One day Bitov and I drank three bottles in the course of a day. But you and Marianna finished a bottle in an hour.

"A new speed record," concluded the writer.

Covering His Private Parts with His Hands

My wife and I went to an exhibition of mine in Zurich.

An excellent room had been reserved for us, in a fine hotel in the center of the city.

Our friend from Paris, the cellist Tolya Liberman, was staying in the same hotel.

We agreed to have dinner together in the hotel restaurant.

When I got back from the gallery, I entered the room. Alesya was taking a bath.

Suddenly the door flew open and a half-naked drug addict, covering his private parts with his hands, moved toward me, bellowing.

Not without difficulty I ejected him and went downstairs to call the police.

A few minutes later, in place of a policeman, appeared a girl administrator in the company of an Italian cook.

The cook held his rolling pin in a threatening manner.

A Gift

In the restaurant, the maitre d' came over and asked us not to make a scene.

For our silence, our table was favored with a gift: a fine bottle of expensive wine.

As he drank, Tolya proposed a plan. We move from one hotel to another.

Following us, he gets undressed and bursts into our room. We call the administrator.

The result: every evening we drink a bottle of excellent wine.

The Sun Shone

In the summer we rented a house on Long Island.

The sun shone, people strolled along the ocean, quick-moving crabs darted in and out of the sand.

Toward evening, my son and I went for a swim and then, anticipating a wonderful dinner, drove off to pick up a bottle of red wine.

Except for us, the liquor store was empty.

The clerk cast a suspicious eye on the two customers speaking an unintelligible language.

Hoping to teach Tyoma about wines, I led him to the section with the most expensive bottles.

Like Ants Were Crawling

Suddenly I felt like ants were crawling up and down my spine.

Sticking my hand in my shorts, to everyone's astonishment, I fished out a live crab, which had chosen an unfortunate place to hide.

In a panic I threw the arthropod on the floor and moved backwards, colliding with the display case of expensive wines.

Holding out his arm, Tyoma averted catastrophe.

Nobody had to call the cops.

We bought our bottle.

Don't Forget the Motherland!

I went to Sardinia to discuss an upcoming artistic project with one of my collectors.

In the morning I decided to go for a swim.

A cheerful little boy was in the water. "Grandpa, Grandpa, let's play submarine!" he shouted, in Russian.

I said hello.

"You live in Moscow?" asked a thickset elderly man, standing waist-deep in the water. He had the face of a Party functionary.

"New York."

"An Englishman?" he asked for some reason, raising his voice.

"No, Russian."

"You go to Russia sometimes?"

"Sometimes."

"Then you're aware that Yalta is only 30 percent booked?"

I was unaware.

"Don't forget the motherland," concluded didactic Grandpa, on his Italian vacation.

Under the Influence of Marxist Ideas

Mama's aunt, Maryaska, emigrated to America before the revolution.

In the 1920s, under the influence of Marxist ideas, the family returned to Russia and settled in Malakhovka with my grandmother.

Unable to tolerate life without a refrigerator or washing machine, they left after one year.

The traces of the American relatives remained hidden in our closet.

Mama, who never threw anything out, would sometimes pull out into full view an old-fashioned American hat or sweater.

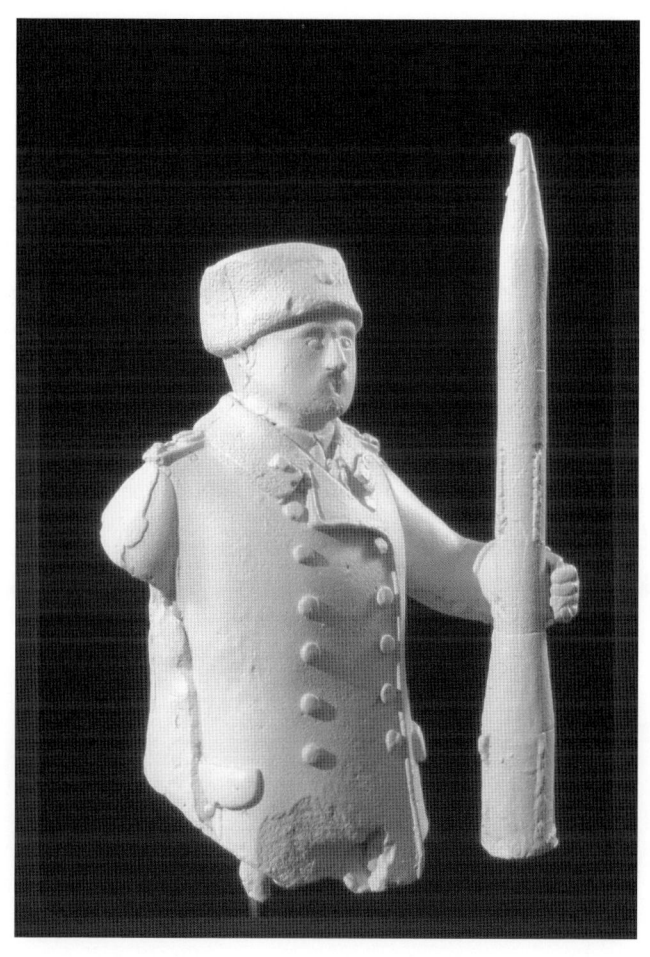

Grisha Bruskin, *General with Missile*
from *An Archeologist's Collection*.

Her Last Wish

In the 1980s, my Uncle Borya received an unexpected letter from abroad.

Maryaska's daughter wrote that her mother had died at a ripe old age in a nursing home.

Before her death, Mama's aunt had called all her children and grandchildren and announced her last wish:

"Go to Russia and find our Russian relatives."

Frightened by Soviet life, Uncle Borya hid the letter and did not answer it.

Her last wish remained unfulfilled.

The Relative

In Russia, all the Bruskins I knew were related to me.

One day in New York, I got a call from an unknown Bruskin. He said he wanted to meet me to put together a family tree. We agreed to have dinner together.

The relative turned out to be a former actor, a very pleasant elderly man with a lively face who reminded me of my grandfathers and uncles.

We passed the evening in great friendliness, like relatives. It turned out that his forebears were from the same place as my father's and that they were engaged in the same business, lumber.

At the end of the evening, the relative, somewhat tipsy, announced that actually his real name was Blyumkin.

When, in the thirties, he began acting on Broadway, he was told that with a Jewish name like that he would never make it. He was advised to change it to something English-sounding, like Ruskin.

My "relative" wanted his new name to start with the familiar letter B.

And that's how he got the name Bruskin.

Dirty Goat

In the summer of 1997, I began work on a porcelain series, *Life Is Everywhere*.

In connection with this project I flew to Petersburg, to establish contact with the Lomonosov Porcelain Factory.

At the same time, the nearby town of Pushkin was holding an arts festival, KukArt. I had been invited, together with my friend the jazz musician Volodya Tarasov, to do a performance called "An Island Is a Piece of Land Surrounded by Water."

Arriving in Petersburg, my wife and I exchanged our "greenies" for rubles and set out for the festival in good spirits. We had a bag of props with us.

First came a ride in the metro.

I waited my turn in line. Holding the heavy bag in one hand, I got out the Russian money with the other hand and held it out to the cashier.

"You bastard," I heard suddenly. "You pig, you goat."

Dumbfounded, I realized after a moment that the voice was coming from behind the cashier's grill, where a strict-looking middle-aged woman was staring me down.

I decided that the long flight had resulted in auditory hallucinations, so I said:

"Excuse me, I don't think I heard you."

"Bastard," she said crisply, drawing out the syllables. "Pig, dirty goat, parasite."

A little overwhelmed, at a loss for why she would be saying this, I asked:

"Excuse me, why are you saying these things?"

"You're supposed to present your bill unfolded," elucidated the voice didactically.

Indeed, I hadn't managed to unfold it.

344

An Authoritative Opinion from Moscow

One time I arrived in Paris two days after the close of Ilya Kabakov's exhibition in the Centre Pompidou.

Regretting that I had missed it, I asked an acquaintance of mine, a Russian artist living there, how he'd liked it.

"You know," he said, "personally I liked it. I didn't expect to. But opinions differ."

"What kind of opinions?" I asked.

"There was an authoritative lady here from Moscow. A critic. People pay a lot of attention to her. So, she has a completely different view."

"What was it?" I asked.

"She looked and said 'no talent,'" concluded my acquaintance with great satisfaction.

A Familiar Question

In 1998, the German government invited me to do a project for the renovated Reichstag.

After many months of work, the project was completed.

In New York, I was asked to give a talk about it.

A Russian woman present in the hall asked a question familiar to me from my former life:

"Moscow has so many talented artists (she named them). Wouldn't you prefer to see someone else in your place?"

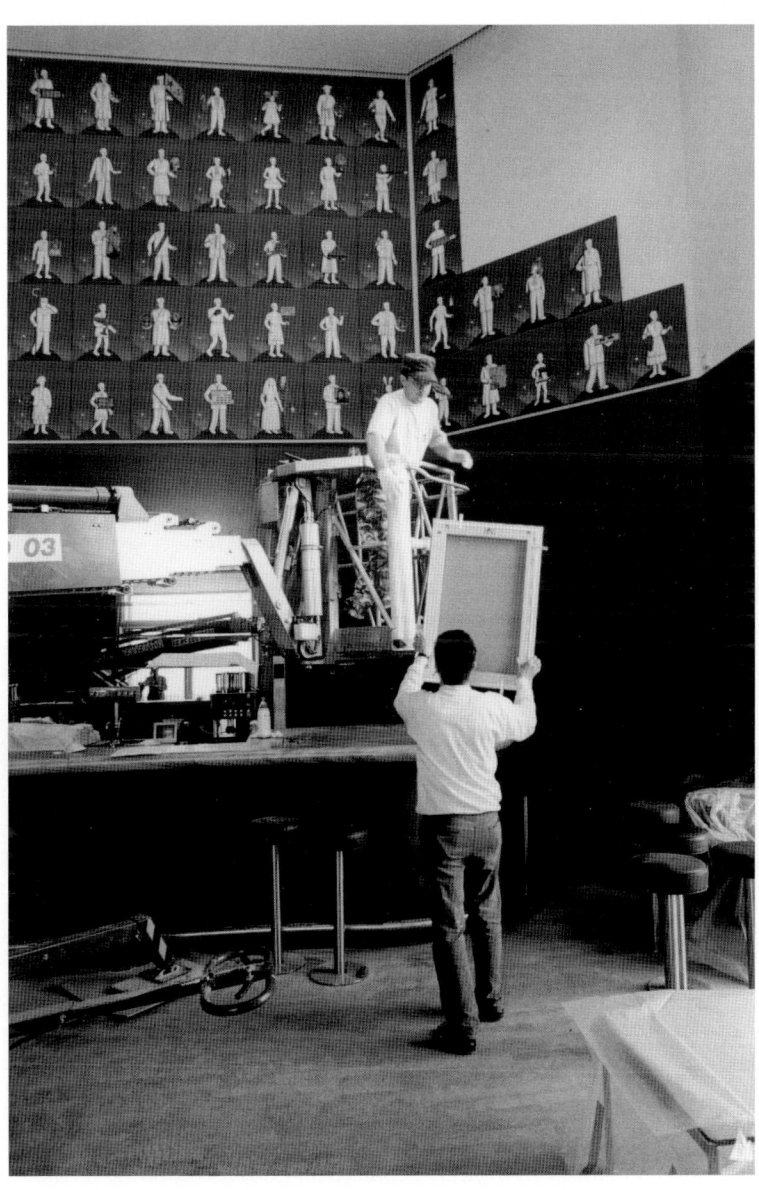

Montage of *Life over All*, Reichstag, Berlin, 1999.
Photograph by Jens Liebchen.

A Focused Vision

Oleg Vasiliev, living in New York, made incredible paintings.

His memory, like vision, focused on the essential.

The result was a clear and pure image of the country where the artist had lived most of his life.

Pierre Levy, seeing one of Vasiliev's best landscapes at my house, said:

"I never was in Russia, but that is exactly the way I have always imagined it."

I'll Tell It Anyway

One day the Vasilievs came to visit.

Sitting at the table, Kira, like a mother, kept nagging Oleg.

"You can't eat this."

"Enough drinking."

Oleg ate and drank everything.

Kira didn't let up.

"Don't tell that story. Nobody's interested."

"I'll tell it anyway," said Oleg, standing his ground.

After which he cut his finger. Getting up, he stumbled and nearly fell over. Returning to his chair, he missed it and landed on the floor.

Kira, as always, had been right.

One Humid Summer Evening

Ernst Neizvestny liked to tell this story:

"One humid summer evening the doorbell rang. I open the door. Andrei Voznesensky. Andrei looks in and without entering, asks:

"'Ernst, when are you coming back to Russia?'"

Ernst had several variants in stock.

"One cold winter evening."

"One dreary autumn evening."

"One warm spring evening."

"Yevgeny Yevtushenko, Robert Rozhdestvensky, Bulat Okuzh-dava . . . "

The Package

I was going to Russia.

Oleg Vasiliev asked me to take a package with a catalog to the poet Vsevolod Nekrasov.

I had always loved his poems. But I was somewhat doubtful about his prose. Reading it, I would be relieved that I didn't know him: the author settled scores with everyone he knew.

When I got to Moscow, I called him right away and said that I had a package for him and that I would call back as soon as I knew my schedule.

A few days later, I did so. Nekrasov expressed his displeasure that I hadn't called earlier.

Easily imagining the kind of treatment I would receive in Seva's next narrative, I decided to keep my distance and passed on the catalog through some mutual friends.

Two Wonderful Artists

In Moscow lived two artists, Shvartsman and Kabakov.
  The two wonderful artists were ideological enemies.
  Shvartsman would say about Kabakov:
  "Art that can be summarized on the telephone is not art."
  Kabakov said about Shvartsman:
  "You can't grab an angel by the ass."

What Did He Say? What Did She Say?

When people came to visit Shvartsman, they knew they were in the presence of a genius.

This knowledge was wholly corroborated by Mikhail Matveevich's esoteric speech and prophetic look.

Earthly life was immaterial to him.

I remember that one visitor offended the master by comparing him to Picasso.

"Picasso was an adolescent," he exclaimed. "A kid in sneakers."

Correcting herself, the guest offered Leonardo Da Vinci.

Mikhail Matveevich did not object.

As I would go downstairs, he would stood on the landing and make the sign of the cross over me.

The next day he'd always call. And sound like a completely different person.

"Who were you with, Grisha?"

"What's she to you?"

"How about the other couple? Are they married or not?"

"And what did he say? What did she say? Is she seeing anybody?" and so on.

Out of False Pride

One time Shvartsman and I had the following telephone conversation.

Shvartsman: "So, Grisha, how's life in the West?"

Me: "Not too bad."

Shvartsman: "That's impossible."

Me: "Why?"

Shvartsman: "Because everybody complains."

Me: "Somehow I haven't heard that."

Shvartsman: "They're lying to you out of false pride."

Untitled

Mikhail Matveevich Shvartsman had never exhibited.

His image was that of a legendary enigmatic genius, who permitted only the initiated to view his works.

A new age dawned.

I ran into him and asked why he was refusing to show his works even now. Mikhail Matveevich said:

"You know, Grisha, I'm afraid to."

He wasn't joking.

In 1994, Shvartsman had made a mistake. He lost his nerve and had an exhibition in the Tretyakov Gallery.

At the opening he was asked to speak.

All Mikhail Matveevich could manage was:

"I . . ."

After a long pause, he got hold of himself and continued:

" . . . am the last remaining . . . "

Whereupon he burst out sobbing.

Young people, a new generation of critics and journalists, took their revenge on this wonderful artist for his reclusive life and reputation as a genius. They called him a "king without any clothes."

Lacking any experience, Shvartsman proved defenseless against the new virus.

This led to his untimely end.

Reality and Dream

In 1997, shortly before Shvartsman's death, my wife and I visited him in Moscow.

After a series of strokes, Mikhail Matveevich was very weak. He spoke a lot about his love for Russia and wept often.

Then he said:

"You know, Kabak calls me every week no matter where he is, and we talk for hours."

Later, in New York, Ilya and Emilia Kabakov came over for dinner. I told Ilya about Shvartsman.

Kabakov said sadly that after he moved to the West he hadn't called Shvartsman a single time.

Apparently for Shvartsman, the philosophical argument with Kabakov was ongoing right up to his death, when reality and dream are indistinguishable.

A Ray of Light

That evening at Shvartsman's there were other guests, Lyuda and
Zhenya Barabanov.

Mikhail Matveevich showed us his photograph.

Gazing from behind the frame was a man who resembled not the
artist but some kind of priest.

A ray of light brightly illuminated his face. Shvartsman said:
"You see, Grisha, this is no accident."

I smirked to myself.

Then we all took pictures, to remember our meeting.

In New York we developed the film.

Everybody turned out sharp and clear except for Shvartsman,
seated in the center.

In every photo, his face melted away in a splotch of light.

The Barabanovs developed their film in Moscow. The same thing
happened.

Masterpiece

At a party at my house in honor of an opening was a couple from Switzerland.

I showed them a collection of paintings by Russian artists, my friends.

The Swiss couple showed no interest.

They paid no attention to superb canvases by Erik Bulatov and Oleg Vasiliev; they walked past early drawings by Ilya Kabakov and wonderful sculptures and objects by Boris Orlov, Lyonya Sokov, and Sasha Kosolapov. They looked indifferently at the best gouaches of Volodya Yakovlev, the marvelous sketches of Mitya Lion, the beautiful paintings of Edik Shteinberg, Ivan Chuikov, Natasha Nesterova, Volodya Nemukhin, Francisco Infante . . .

Suddenly they stirred, and I finally saw on their faces the enthusiasm I had been waiting for.

Taking a small study of an orange on a blue background, they began praising the masterpiece in ecstatic terms.

The painter of this masterpiece was my assistant's daughter.

Her mother was thinking of sending the girl to art school and brought an example of her work to get my opinion.

The Hero of a Nightmare

In August 1999 I was about to fly back from Moscow.

Not trusting the post office, I turned into a personal cargo carrier. The artworks for my porcelain project *Life Is Everywhere* had been made in Russia, and I needed to take them to an exhibition at the Marlborough Gallery.

I successfully passed through Russian customs, looking the inspector straight in his penetrating eyes.

When I reached passport control, the border guard announced that the Russian Foreign Ministry had just declared my Russian passport, valid until 2001, null and void. And I, like the hero of some emigrant's nightmare, could not leave the country without renewing it.

A Russian Face

The opening was to take place in three days.

Loading my stuff into a car, I ran around the city in a panic, trying to get a new passport.

When I had been photographed, I compared the picture to the one on my American passport.

The American color print showed a well-groomed, self-assured, thoroughly likable citizen.

The Russian black-and-white revealed a wild-haired man with beady eyes, a character from the popular Soviet film *Operation Y.*

I understood that Russian life creates the Russian face.

As the Soul Soars over the Abyss

Mama passed away as I was flying to Israel to say farewell to her.

She was buried in a Jewish cemetery on one of the Jerusalem hills.

The grave site was at the edge of a cliff, at the height of flying birds.

During the ceremony I saw a falcon soaring above the abyss at the level of my face, around four yards away from the open grave.

The bird hung motionless in the sky—and I, on the earth.

Mama was buried, and the bird disappeared.

Herald

A few months later, the city of Raanana in Israel asked me to install a sculpture in one of the city parks.

I thought about my mother.

I agreed.

The project was completed. The sculpture was put in place.

I flew to Israel and went with my family to Raanana.

From afar I saw a falcon. Making a circle, it alighted on the statue as if waiting for us.

Letting the visitors get within a few feet, the herald slowly rose into the sky and flew off.

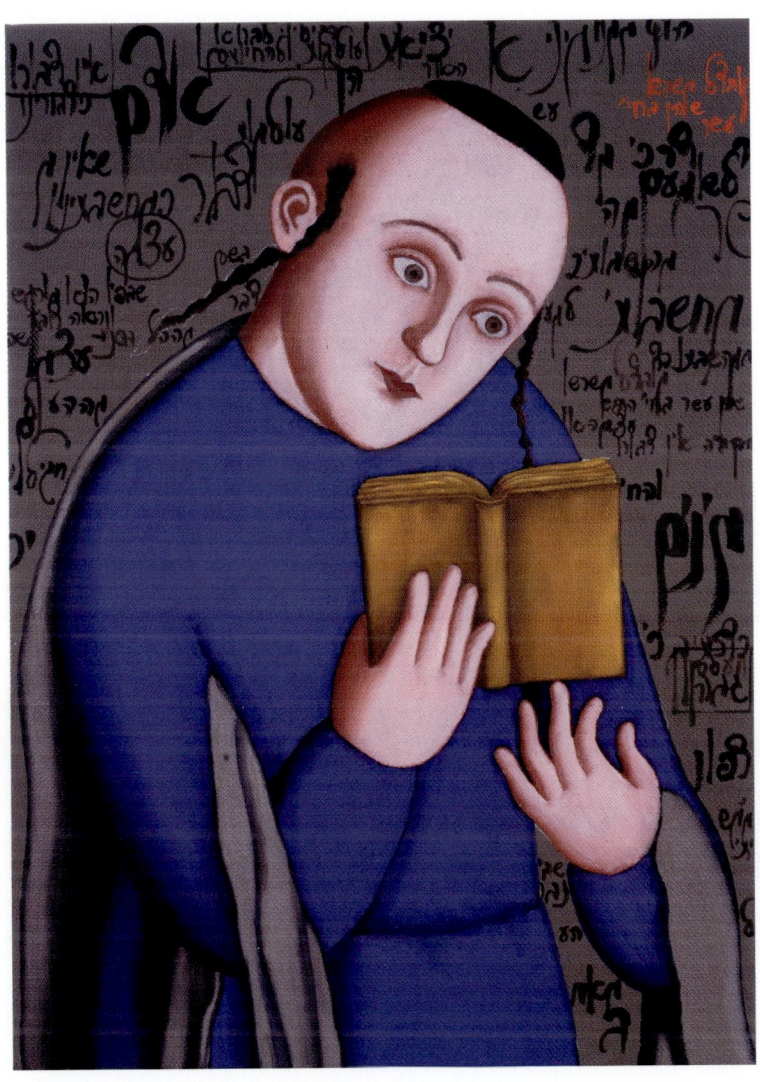

Grisha Bruskin, *Alefbet* (fragment), oil on linen.

Post Scriptum

From time to time I would go from New York to Israel to visit my parents.

As we said good-bye, Mama always said the same thing:

"Once again there was no time for a good talk."

Every time, I had the feeling that the most important talk was still to come.

I often see Mama in my dreams. She smiles at me:

"You see, Grisha, finally no one is disturbing us, and you and I can have a good, quiet talk about everything."

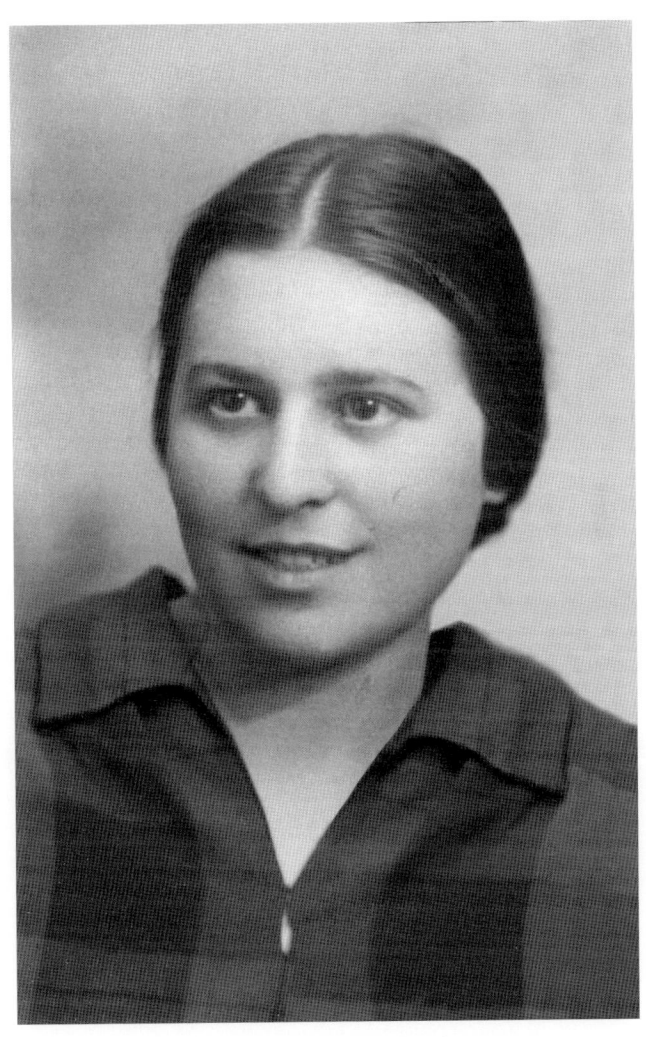

My mother in her youth.